MW00942177

Thawing Adult/Child Syndrome
and other Codependent Patterns

www.Internet-of-the-Mind.com
Email: dcarter73@msn.com
Phone: (573) 634-2254

Or Write to:
Don Carter, MSW, LCSW
83 South Larand Dr.
Lake MyKee
Holts Summit, MO 65043

TABLE OF CONTENTS

Section 3: Getting to know your True Self

Chapter 1

"What the hell is wrong with you?"

Comedian Bill Cosby has often observed that one of a child's most frequent answers to questions posed by their parents is "I don't know." He forgets to mention that one of a parent's most frequent questions to their children is some variation of *"What the hell is wrong with you?"* I always hated that question. How was I supposed to answer it? ... *"Well, Dad, I'm very happy you asked because I think we really need to talk about this. You see, my childhood dependency needs have not been getting met lately and, as a result, I am suffering from a pretty bad case of low self-esteem and some abandonment issues. If you could see your way clear to lighten up on me a bit I might have a chance to get back on track."* I doubt that would have gone over very well.

I am not sure that my alternative approach was much better for my own kids. I modified the question into a little game. When I found myself wanting to ask one of them, *"What the hell is wrong with you?"* I would stop, raise an eyebrow just a bit, look at them for a moment, and then curiously inquire, *"What grade are you in?"* They would give the answer to which I would smile and say, *"Oh ... that explains it! Maybe they don't teach you about this until next year."*

Motivation

Motivation has been defined as a drive, a need, a desire to do something. In human beings, motivation involves both conscious and unconscious drives. It is this writer's belief that people all have one *ultimate* motive in common. This motive drives everything we think, everything we feel, and everything we do from the time we wake in the morning until we go to sleep at night. I believe this motive is simply to be happy.

In this case, the term *happiness* does not necessarily refer to a feeling or emotion. Feelings come and go so it is not realistic (nor desirable) to hope to stay in one emotional state.

Rather, used in this context, happiness is more like a universal *state of being* that describes and contains other states of being such as: contentment, satisfaction, fulfillment, completeness, and wholeness. Again, it is this *pursuit of happiness that is at the root of everything we think, everything we feel, and everything we do.* We all have this same ultimate goal in common, and we are all doing the best we can with what we have to get as close to that ideal as possible. If all of our efforts fail, and we move too far away from the ideal then things can go very wrong, as in the case of someone who can feel empty, unhappy, and unmotivated.

As our ultimate goal in life, the desire to be happy motivates us to make decisions based upon what will move us closer to the positive end of a continuum. On the negative end of this continuum is pain, something we try very hard to stay away from. Most of us do not like pain, but it does have a very important role in our lives. Pain is a warning system that tells us when we are moving in the wrong direction, taking us further away from our ultimate goal.

Granted, we sometimes purposefully make decisions that we know are going to hurt, in the short-term anyway. However, even these painful decisions are driven by the desire to be happy because we know that in the long run we will gain from the short-term pain. For example, deciding not to marry the person of our dreams until we finish college and get our finances in order may be painful in the short-term but very rewarding in the long run. It may even play a part in whether the marriage succeeds or fails. When we make decisions like this, we are said to be mature because we can delay gratification.

There are other times we make decisions that don't make us happy such as when we act without hesitating long enough to think it through. For example, impulsively taking out a new line of credit or buying a new car when we cannot afford it may provide some instant gratification but soon leads to buyer's remorse and other negative long-term consequences when the bills start coming in. Buyer's remorse is an example of an emotional consequence we suffer when we realize what we have done and how it is going to lead to our future unhappiness. When we don't stop and think it through before we act, we are said to have impulse control problems, a sign of immaturity.

When immaturity persists into adulthood it suggests that some sort of developmental delay has taken place such as emotional arrest. Developmental delays are usually the consequence of unmet childhood needs. Frozen feeling-states are another way of describing these developmental issues. We will explore these concepts in great detail throughout this book. We will also explore a very simple, yet incredibly powerful formula, A → B (→ = leads to). This formula is where A is a choice we make and B is the outcome. The outcome is where we find ourselves on the pleasure and pain continuum as a consequence of our choice.

Maslow's Hierarchy

The American psychologist Abraham Maslow (1968) devised a six-level hierarchy of needs that, according to his theory, drive human behavior. I believe that each of these needs must be met in order for one to truly be happy. Maslow progressively ranks human needs as follows:

1. Physiological - food, shelter, clothing;
2. Security and safety;
3. Love and feelings of belonging;
4. Competence, prestige, and esteem;
5. Curiosity and the need to know; and
6. Self-Actualization

Maslow suggests that each preceding need must be met, at least to some degree, before one can go on to the next level. For instance, a child may not be able to pay attention in class if she is preoccupied with hunger. Maslow refers to the first four levels as deficiency needs and the last two growth needs.

While these needs are important for all human beings, special attention must be given to how we meet these needs in children because, as we shall see, it is the meeting of these needs, or not meeting them, that sets in motion a whole series of events that have an impact on the adjustment of that child. In children, deficiency needs are also referred to as dependency needs because children cannot meet these needs themselves; they *depend* upon their caretakers to meet these needs for them.

Childhood Dependency Needs

Small children cannot meet their own needs, much like a plant cannot water itself. As we grow, we become more *independent* and able to meet more and more of our needs on our own. There are two groups of dependency needs. The first group is the survival needs. These are what Maslow calls the basic needs for food, shelter, clothing, medical attention, safety and protection. If these needs are not met, at least to a minimal degree, the child is likely to die. Notice that the survival needs include the child's need to feel safe and protected. If a child does not feel safe she cannot relax. She is always on guard, scanning her environment for danger. Her anxiety level is very high, and she has to stay alert and "tuned in" to everything going on around her causing her to become hyper-vigilant, hyper-alert, and/or hyper-sensitive. Feeling safe helps children relax; if they can't relax they can't play. If they can't play it interferes with their growth. Play is how children learn and grow along normal developmental lines.

Because feeling safe is so important, children have a built-in psychological defense mechanism called idealization which functions to help them feel safe. This is necessary for them to be able to relax enough to play which, again, is the business of being a child. Through idealization, children (not referring to teenagers here) set their parents up on a pedestal, seeing them as godlike creatures. This makes them feel safe because "if I am protected by a godlike creature and then nothing can get to me" (Bradshaw). Of course children cannot yet think that way, but they "get it" that way in an emotional sense. We will come back to idealization later.

The emotional dependency needs are what Maslow refers to as the basic needs for love and esteem. These are the needs that nourish a child emotionally. If they get these needs met fully on a consistent basis, children thrive and flourish. If they don't get these needs met, they suffer to an extent proportional to their lack of need fulfillment. John Bradshaw (1992, 2005) refers to the following as primary emotional dependency needs: *Time*, *Attention*, *Affection*, and *Direction*.

Time = Love

Bradshaw and others point out that a small child equates time with love. In his video *Shame and Addiction*, Bradshaw states, "Little kids get it that whatever their parents give their time to is what they love." So if dad is gone working ten to twelve hours a day, which may be his way of showing love, the kids feel that dad loves what he is doing more than he loves them. They don't understand about budgets and bills. They don't understand that this may be dad's way of demonstrating his love for the family. All they know is he is usually gone and when he comes home, he is too tired to spend time with them. All he wants to do is rest, read the paper, and watch some TV. The main point here is that the children need time from *both* parents, not just one. They need enough time from each parent to get the message that they are loved as much as anyone else in the family. It is not as much of a question of quantity as it is of consistency and quality. "Quality time" is when the child's other three emotional needs are also being met.

Attention = Worth

Just as children equate time with love, they get it that attention equals worth or value. Attention is more than just listening to the children; it is *attending* to them. Parents attend to children when they take them seriously, show genuine concern and curiosity about who they are, what they think, how they feel. Attentive parents notice when the child is struggling with a feeling and help figure out what it is and what to do about it. They are engaged in their child's life, to the extent that they know how their child's day went, who the child is hanging out with, what the highlight of the week was, etc.

Children need lots of attention, and if they don't get it their behavior becomes attention-seeking. This is not deliberate on their part. Most of the time, children really don't know why they act-out in ways that are obviously designed to get attention. They are compelled to do it because they *need* attention, not because they *want* attention. When was the last time you heard this statement, "Oh, he's trying to get attention, just ignore him." Sometimes this is bad advice, other times it is not. There are two reasons kids show attention-seeking behavior: when they are not getting enough attention, and when they have been used to getting too much attention. The latter will be discussed when we look at the need for direction.

Affection = Approval

As a therapist, it has been my experience that affection is the area where many families seem to fall short. Many of my clients have told me, "Well, mine were not the most affectionate parents in the world, but I always knew they loved me." I am sure it is true that they were loved. However, I am also aware that kids need hugs, kisses, pats on the back, and words of encouragement on a regular basis. Displays of affection are how approval messages are sent from the parent to the child. Affection says "I like you," "I like who you are and who you are becoming," "I am glad you are my child," "I am happy I get to be your parent," "I am grateful we have been blessed with you." In other words, affection is how children get the message that they are approved of by the parent. How many of us know a child who is not sure what his father thinks of him? Or one who is uncertain whether she measures up to her mother's expectations? How many are sure that we *don't* measure up?

Kids who don't get enough affection display approval-seeking behaviors such as people-pleasing. They act-out their need for approval by trying to please mom or dad. When their attempts go un-noticed they try harder and harder to please them, setting in motion the development of an ingrained pattern of people-pleasing behavior. We will look more at these types of behavioral patterns later.

Direction:

Guidance = Competence

Children are born not knowing how to do things. They are biologically programmed to survive in the wild, but everything about how to live in our culture must be learned, including relationships. Our caretakers are our teachers. Dad shows us how to be a man in the world; Mom shows us how to be a woman in the world; and they both show us how men and women get along with each other. In other words, our cultural and interpersonal programming is not biologically endowed but comes through the modeling of our parents, whether they realize it or not.

In the ideal situation, parents do realize the powerful influence their behavior has on the development of their children. They also know that to be good teachers they have to be available and approachable: i.e., the children know when and where to find dad or mom, and they know that it is okay to go to them for advice and assistance. To be available goes back to the issues of time and attention, parents must make the time to attend to the questions of their kids. To be approachable they must also be patient, tolerant, and affectionate. Good teachers understand that kids need repetition to learn. They may have to ask and be shown more than once in order to develop competence at a certain task.

A sense of competence and mastery are critical to the development of a child's sense of self. For instance, when parents teach a child to ride a bike, they hold on and hold on until the child gets her balance, and then they let go. Usually, the child will crash a time or two, but soon she takes off and rides. Did you ever see children who take off on a bike for the first time? They light up like a Christmas tree and almost universally shout the same thing: *"Look at me! I'm doing it!"* This is a statement of competence and provides a huge boost to their ego. After a while, you might hear the same child shout, *"Look at me! I'm doing it with no hands!"* This shows that the child now has a sense of mastery. Do you ever wonder why kids do the same thing repeatedly once they become proficient at it and avoid things they might not do well? Satisfying the need for a sense of competence and mastery is the reason. Children need as many I-can-do-it experiences as we can give them. Things like tying their shoe for the first time, driving a car, going on a date, learning to dance, getting good grades, learning to cook, hitting a baseball, etc.

Parents help their kids get the I-can-do-it experience by helping them develop the skill sets necessary to perform a given task. This again requires time, attention, and affection. If children learn the fundamentals of something, they are much more likely to succeed. If they try to learn on their own, without any ideas of the fundamentals, they are likely to fail more times than they need to. Kids who fail too much eventually give up trying. They need available and approachable teachers to help them learn.

Approachable teachers help without resorting to criticism when working with a child. It is truly an art, and most of us were raised on criticism so it is difficult to learn. Healthy critical feedback comes with love, tolerance, and without shame. For example, helpful criticism might sound like this: "I know it's difficult." "You are doing very well …I fell off more than this when I was your age." "I know you can do it, let's try one more time for today." Shameful criticism sounds like this: "Oh come on, don't be a big baby!" "You always make things harder than they should be." "Your brother took off on his first try … are you going let him make you look bad?"

One other issue regarding guidance is *over-protection,* which must also be explored here. There are some families that have rigid, sometimes extremely over-controlling rules designed to "protect" the child. For example, "The training wheels don't come off until you are twelve years old," "You cannot climb trees," "You can go outside but don't do anything," and "You must wear a football helmet if you are going to get on the swing set." They also do everything for the child, even that which children should be able to do themselves. Over-protection and over-involvement is a result of a parent's inability to tolerate any chance that their child might get hurt, physically or emotionally (failure). This can easily be mistaken for love, when, in fact, it is not. This is more about the parent's need to feel safer than it is about the child's need for protection. The child not only misses out on the I-can-do-it experiences but also gets a message from the god-like creatures in his life that *he can't do it*–a feeling of incompetence is the result. The child feels *"If Mom and Dad don't think I can do it, then I must not be able to do it."* These kids usually end up with all kinds of problems with indecision, shame, fear, and anxiety.

Discipline = Character

Discipline is the second form of direction kids need. Children are born without the internal structures to control their own impulses. Therefore, they were given external structures, called parents, to help them. When parents set limits for their children they are telling them "Here's the line, if you step over it this is what happens" (A → B). Setting and enforcing good limits helps develop the internal structures necessary for children to control their own impulses. These structures build character. Character consists of two primary internal structures: *values*–the knowledge of right and wrong, and *self-discipline*–the ability to delay or deny the gratification of impulses based upon that knowledge.

If we remember a simple formula, A → B, then we will have quite a bit of knowledge about setting good limits. Cause-and-effect seems to be a law of the universe. Simply put, when our *behavior* (A) is a good thing, then the *outcome* (B) should also a good thing; when A is a bad thing, then B should also a bad thing. The consequences we receive (positive or negative) shape our behaviors by reinforcing the good and dissuading the bad. While this formula is simple in theory, it is difficult in practice because this life does not always go as it "should," as we shall see in the next chapter.

Healthy limits are firm, effective, and consistent. The limits (B) are also connected and proportionate to the behavior (A); i.e., let the punishment fit the crime. When parents set and consistently enforce good limits for their children, they are teaching an important law of the universe. This will be extremely significant to children later in their adulthood when life becomes their teacher. Conversely, when we are inconsistent with the limits, or they are inappropriate for the behavior, then we are doing our children a huge disservice. For instance, when a teenager does "A" (e.g., comes home smelling of alcohol), and they should receive "B" (e.g., grounded for a certain period of time) but the parent feels sorry for them because the prom is this weekend, so they provide "C" (Letting them off the hook and giving them $50 to have a good time) then the message sent and received is A → C, In other words, "If I screw up when it really counts, Mom and Dad will bail me out." Providing "C" when "B" should follow interferes with the grand design, *enabling* problem behaviors to persist.

Decisions about good limits are not always easy. Some limits must be nonnegotiable, e.g. those related to the safety of the child and those connected with strongly held family values, while others can be structured to teach the child flexibility and how to compromise. For example, when the child does "A" (breaks curfew by thirty minutes *for the first time ever*), and the agreed upon consequence is "B" (grounded for the next two weekends) the negotiated agreement might be that the child can choose which two weekends of the next month to be grounded.

Another word for limits is boundaries. When parents set and consistently enforce healthy limits, they are helping their child learn healthy boundaries. Children who don't know where the boundaries are tend to feel unsafe. Spoiled-child syndrome is what results when a child is given blanket approval for everything he or she does. When there are little or no consequences provided for these children, they push the limits and push the limits until someone steps in to say "no!" Misbehavior in this case is *discipline-seeking* behavior. The child is unconsciously acting-out his *need* for help with controlling his impulses, and they are compelled to get it. Just as in over-protection, the well-meaning intentions of the over-indulgent parent backfire. Usually, the parents are trying very hard not to hurt the child's self-esteem with criticism, so they rarely provide this form of protection. The child gets the message that the god-like creatures in his life have no expectations of him because they are not capable of living up to any expectations due to incompetence.

Other forms of discipline include the ones that moms and dads model for us in their own daily behavior, including good manners, hygiene, work ethics, etc. We watch and learn from them. The old adage *"Do as I say, not as I do"* is not very effective in helping our kids develop and internalize these daily disciplines. The most effective tool in teaching kids is good role-modeling. Limits and consequences simply reinforce what we demonstrate.

The Iceberg Model

Throughout the book, I will refer to *the Iceberg Model* [Fig.1] to develop a picture or roadmap of what happens when childhood dependency needs go unmet. The Iceberg Model has been used as a visual tool to simplify very abstract concepts of being human by many people, including Sigmund Freud, Friel and Friel, and Dr. Larry Crabb, to name a few. You will hear many of the ideas and principles of the pioneers in the field of addiction theory such as Charles Whitfield MD, John Bradshaw, Pia Mellody, Vernon Johnson, Claudia Black, Terrence Gorski, and many others. They have been my teachers on such topics as addiction, codependency, Adult/Child Syndrome, abandonment, shame, and childhood dependency needs. I have used the Iceberg to integrate some of their ideas, along with many of my own, into this unified model of the issues underlying most addictive, mental, emotional, interpersonal, and even spiritual problems. To delve deeper into many of the concepts presented here see Appendix A for a list of suggested readings.

It has been my experience that most people have a profound revelation about who they are, where they came from, and where they can go from here after hearing the Iceberg lecture. It is my hope that this book will produce the same results for you, the reader. Again, the best thing about this model is that it keeps some very abstract ideas relatively simple and provides a concrete roadmap for understanding and preparing for change. So let's get started …

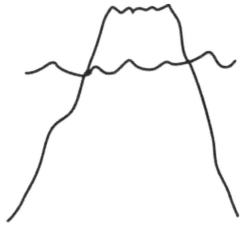

Figure 1: Iceberg Model

The Iceberg represents a human being. The waterline represents the dividing line between what is in our consciousness or awareness (above) and what is in our unconsciousness or our unawareness (below). The deeper one looks beneath the surface symbolizes the deeper we are into our unawareness or our unconscious. It is my hope readers will have a better idea of how to achieve that one "ultimate motive," which we all have in common by the time they have finished reading.

Please, if you are a parent, as you read, try to focus on at least as much of your own childhood experience as you do on the experience of your children. This book is not about blaming parents because, as we shall discuss later, the vast majority of parents do the best they can with what they are given. If you are reading this book, chances are that sometime in the past you have said something like, *"My kids are going to have it better than I did!"* This statement is an affirmation that you understand what it is like not to get your dependency needs met, at least to some degree.

Chapter 2

Anatomy of an Emotional Wound

According to Linn, Fabricant, and Linn (1988), in the early 1900s if you were born into an orphanage in the United States you were likely to be dead by the time you were two years old. This was according to a study done by Dr. Henry Chapin, a pediatrician in New York City. There was another pediatrician, Dr. Fritz Talbot, who found those statistics unacceptable. He discovered an orphanage in Dusseldorf, Germany where the mortality rate was the same as the general population, so he went to investigate. The doctor found that the orphanage followed very similar policies and procedures as those here in America with one small difference. There was an older woman named Anna, who carried a child on each hip. The director of the orphanage told Dr. Talbot, "When we have done everything medically possible for a baby, and it is still not doing well, we turn the child over to old Anna. Whenever a child cried the woman would pick the child up, hold him or her, and give motherly love. A few minutes with old Anna literally meant the difference between life and death for some kids."

When this doctor came back to the United States, he shared his findings and several institutions recruited volunteers to do the same things Anna did. Not surprisingly in a very short time the mortality rate quickly became consistent with the general population.

Abandonment

Children who get their dependency needs met fully on a regular basis will thrive, flourish, and grow at a healthy pace. Life will be good for these kids. In the worst-case scenario, kids who do not get their needs met at all will experience a failure to thrive, and many will die. Let us use the analogy of an emotional gas tank; if our needs are met fully we feel full, complete, satisfied, content, and happy. If we don't get our needs met at all we feel a great emptiness inside. I have heard this emptiness described in many ways: a black hole, a void, a vacuum, an ache, or a longing. Perhaps we get our needs met half-way; we feel half-full but something is missing, and we still feel an ache. These are emotional wounds, also known as *original pain*, and they result from an *abandonment* of our childhood dependency needs.

A Word about Blame

When parents do not meet the needs of their children, it is not usually because the parents don't love them. I say "usually" because there are those cases that one cannot understand, accept, explain, or excuse for any reason. However, most parents do the best they can, given the internal and external resources they possess, to take care of their children. In fact, I cannot count the times I have heard parents say, "I try hard to make sure my kids have it better than I did." This speaks very loudly to me. It says that these parents are familiar with unmet dependency needs. So, most often, it is not the parent's lack of love or effort that is to blame. It is usually because of one of the following reasons that abandonment occurs:

1. Circumstances: For example, if one parent dies and the other must take two jobs to care for ten children, circumstances are to blame for this, not the parents. None-the-less the children get hurt in the process.

2. Wounded people wound people: Parents cannot demonstrate much more than they have been given. Our parents were raised by their parents who likely were also wounded, and they were raised by their parents, etc. Maybe dad is an alcoholic; he has a disease that impaired his ability function in his major life roles, including his ability to be the kind of father his kids need him to be. He did not aspire to become alcoholic. Alcoholism chooses you, you don't choose it. Perhaps mom is so chronically depressed she can't leave a dark room much less take care of anyone else; she didn't choose that. However, the primary issue for parents is

that they are wounded themselves, sometimes moderately, other times severely because their parents were also wounded, and their parents were wounded, etc. Whatever the issue, the result is wounded children.

Again, it is not usually a question of whether our parents loved us, or even if they did the best they could for us. Many people get stuck on this truth and end up saying, "So why go back and dig all that up? They did the best they could and that is that. You can't change the past." To those people, I say keep reading, this book will show you why it is important to "dig all that up." Suffice it to say here that assigning blame is *not* the reason.

Children have not yet developed the skills to cope effectively with emotional pain. It seems they can handle a broken arm better than a broken heart. They rely heavily on a defense mechanism called repression to push the emotional wound deep into their unawareness [Fig. 2]. They also act-out their pain in various ways as a survival instinct which calls attention to it so the adults in their life can assess, diagnose, and respond to them. If the adults are unresponsive, and the child continues to experience abandonment the wounds accumulate.

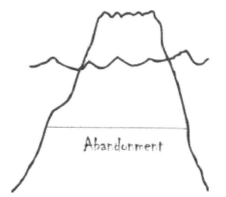

Abandonment

Figure 2: The wound of abandonment

The extent of the wounds may be mild, moderate, or severe depending upon the extent of the abandonment. Mild to moderate cases of wounding comes from situations in which the child does not fully or consistently get their emotional dependency needs met. There may be few overt signs of family dysfunction or abuse. For instance, it may be that one or both parents are able to give reasonable amounts time, attention and direction but are unable to express affection. The words *"I love you"* may rarely be heard, if at all, in this family. A lack of hugs, kisses, and other forms of emotional warmth leave a child to wonder how they measure up in the eyes of their parents. It makes matters even worse when the child lives in a shame-based family system. In such families the children get messages of disapproval through constant criticism rather than messages of approval and warmth.

A shame-based family system is characterized by the parent's use of shame to provide direction to the child. For instance, when a five-year-old child scrapes his knee the parent, or parents, might tell the child to stop crying because *"Big boys don't cry."* They may also simply ignore the child until he or she stops crying. Similarly, when the child makes a mistake the parent might say, *"What's wrong with you?"* or *"Why can't you be more like your sister?"*

Sometimes the shaming goes to extremes, especially when a wounded, shame-based parent is angry: *"You are going to end up in prison!"* *"You'll never amount to anything!"* *"You never were any good; why do you do this to me?"* These comments are often accompanied by slaps or even punches from the parent. In shame-based families these types of comments and behaviors are often intended to "help" the child learn right from wrong. However, while the intended "help" may actually produce the intended result the next time, another result is emotional wounds for the child. Shame is discussed in more detail in the next section of this chapter.

Another common abandonment scenario occurs when one of the parents is physically absent much of the time. The parent may be a "workaholic" who cannot seem to stop working long enough to find time for his family. The workaholic rationalizes his absence and breaks promises to be there for the child in the same way an alcoholic rationalizes her drinking and breaks promises to stop or control it better.

By now, the reader may begin to suspect that abandonment and wounding must happen on some level to most, if not all, of us. I believe it is true that all of us experience emotional wounds in life, but *not all of us* experience abandonment. The best example is when we lose someone or something important to us. Grief is a natural part of living, and one cannot escape an encounter with it for long in this world. When someone or something becomes important to us, we bond with it on an emotional level. Emotional wounds result when this bond is breaking or broken. Grief is the process we must go through to let go of the attachment and heal from the resulting loss-related emotional wound.

The absence of a parent may be perfectly justifiable as when a military parent is abruptly deployed overseas for a year or longer. As already mentioned, little kids get it that parents love what they give their time to. So if the child gets little or no time from a parent, the child tends to *experience it* as little or no love, regardless of the reason for the absence. Whether or not it results in abandonment in the case of circumstantial, unavoidable, or justifiable absences, such as the above example of deployment, is determined by what happens before, during, and after the absence of the parent.

There has been much written that suggests the terms "abandonment" and "loss" are interchangeable. While both result in emotional wounds, the author believes they are not interchangeable terms and that an important distinction must be made. *Abandonment always involves loss for the child, but loss does not always involve abandonment.* Loss-related wounds can heal if the person possesses the psychological support and emotional coping skills necessary to aid in the grieving process. Children who have emotionally healthy, responsive parents tend to get their needs met consistently. Because of that, they are equipped either internally with their own coping skills (depending on their age) and/or externally with parents who are able to provide the necessary support through the grief process.

When children cannot put into words what they are experiencing, whether it be from abandonment or other significant losses, their pain must find expression somehow and does so through *compulsive* patterns of behavior commonly referred to as "acting-out." When their needs are going unmet, children are *compelled by instinct* to act-out their needs through behaviors designed to elicit an appropriate response from caregivers, provided the caregivers are able to respond appropriately. If it is attention he need, the child's behavior will be attention-seeking. If they need approval, the behavior will be approval-seeking. And if the child needs discipline his behavior will likely be discipline-seeking. It is as if the child is an actor in a play, hence the term "acting-out." There are some clearly defined patterns of acting-out that not only help children find expressions for their pain but also actually help them to survive. We will discuss these patterns of behavior, better known as survival roles, in greater detail in the next chapter.

As already mentioned, young children do not possess the necessary skills to cope with emotional pain on their own. As with everything else they are dependent on their caretakers for help in grieving. The best children can do is to act-out their pain and hope their parents and other caretakers in their lives are healthy enough to notice the behavior, accurately assess the need, and respond accordingly. When parents possess the skills to respond consistently to their children's needs for time, attention, affection, and direction, they are helping their children resolve the current episode of grief to some extent, as well as to build the internal structures necessary to cope effectively with grief and loss on their own later in life. When parents are not able to respond appropriately to the child's need for help, loss-related wounds tend to accumulate right along with the wounds of abandonment, further complicating the child's pain.

Severe cases of emotional wounding, also known as trauma, results in situations where children have experienced overt abuse or other major losses coupled with inadequate support to aid in their grief. The emotional trauma that comes from abuse violates not only the child's emotional dependency needs but also his most basic needs, the survival dependency needs. This is especially true for their need to feel safe and protected. Imagine a child's dilemma when he needs protection from the very people who are supposed to provide it. The following are some forms of abuse and/or major losses that produce moderate to severe emotional trauma in children:

Sexual and Physical Abuse

Emotional abuse or neglect: Emotionally unavailable parent(s) or parents who give their child the opposite of what they need such as name-calling, belittling, threats of abandonment, shaming, etc.

Psychological abuse: Ignoring the child as if she does not exist or denial of a child's reality such as telling her they didn't see what she saw (e.g., "Daddy wasn't drunk, don't you ever say that again!")

- Frequent Moves
- Adoption Issues
- Prolonged separation from a parent
- Reversal of parent/child roles
- Rigid family rules
- Divorce
- Death of a parent or other family member
- Mentally Ill parent or family member
- Cruel and Unusual punishment: such as locking a child in the closet.

Shame

As discussed in Chapter 1, it is imperative that children feel safe and protected as part of getting their survival needs met. In order to feel safe, even in an unsafe environment, children idealize their caretakers. In other words, little kids put their parents up on a pedestal and see them as perfect, all-knowing and all-powerful god-like creatures. Idealization is a defense mechanism that helps children feel safe because they get the feeling that nothing can get to them, since they are protected by a god.

Since god-like creatures are perfect, they are beyond reproach in the innocent mind of a child. Children cannot say to themselves, *"Well, Dad has a drinking problem. That's about him not me; I don't have to take it personally when he breaks his promises and yells at me all the time."* No, in the mind of a child it goes more like this… *"If I were a better kid Daddy wouldn't drink."* or *"If I was a better kid Mommy wouldn't yell at me so much."* or the classic, *"Daddy, please don't leave, I'll be good!"*

Because of idealization, young children can make sense of it no other way; it has to be about them. Parents have all the power, and the child has none. They are totally submitted and committed to the parent. Thus, they develop a sense of defectiveness, and it begins to grow along with the wounds. So, if abandonment is an emotional wound, then *shame is an emotional infection* that sets in as the wound goes unattended [see Fig. 3]. This infection has a voice, and it grows stronger as the wounds accumulate. The child's self-talk begins to sound like this, *"No one could ever love me."* *"I don't count."* *"What's wrong with me?"* *"I'm stupid, lazy, unworthy of anyone's attention."*

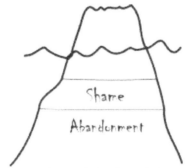

Figure 3: The infection of shame

In a shame-based family system, these internal messages of shame are actually confirmed by the parents. Sometimes the confirmations are more subtle and come in veiled threats of abandonment, double-bind messages, gestures that convey contempt for the child and other nonverbal expressions of disdain. Other times the confirmations are directly stated through name-calling, belittling, and emotional battering such as *"You're stupid, ugly, lazy, fat,"* etc. *"No one could love you." "You can't do anything right."* These messages result in what John Bradshaw (2005) has termed "toxic shame" in his book *Healing the Shame that Binds You*. Of course, these messages frequently come with a misguided positive intention to motivate the child.

The infection of shame exacerbates the wounds of abandonment, and the pain grows. In the worst-case scenarios, such as sexual abuse or incest, toxic shame is a byproduct regardless of the messages a child received before the abuse occurred, or after it ended.

Contempt

In keeping with the analogy of a wound, *contempt is the scab* that forms over the infection of shame and the wound of abandonment [see Fig. 4]. The scab of contempt consists of all the "crusty" feelings of anger, resentment, and bitterness. It is what the child is most aware of, and it skews his whole experience of life as well as his role in it. Some call it the "life sucks" syndrome. The negative energy from the contempt must be directed somewhere. There are two possible choices, and the choice is made at an unconscious level. The energy can be directed inward in the form of self-contempt; or outward as contempt for people, society, authority figures, the opposite sex, or whoever is available, including God.

If we have a tendency to point the contempt inward at self, we are *internalizing* it. If we are more likely to turn it outward toward others, we are e*xternalizing* the contempt. The self-talk of an Internalizer is all about the defectiveness of self and his or her unworthiness to exist, leading to inappropriate guilt, and more shame, making the emotional infection worse. The self-talk of the Externalizer is all about the defectiveness of others and the unfairness of it all, leading to inappropriate anger.

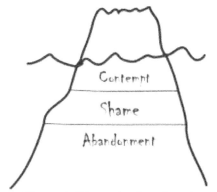

Figure 4: The scab of contempt

Many of us will internalize the contempt until we can't take it anymore and then blow up, directing it outward in an attempt to ventilate. When we externalize or "dump" our contempt it lands on whoever is nearby, usually those who are closest to us. Then, because we have hurt someone we love, we turn the contempt back on ourselves through more shame-based messages such as, *"See there. I've done it again ... I've hurt someone I care about! I've proven it this time ... I really am a loser!"* Internalizing the contempt feeds the infection of shame, speeding up its progression and the power it has over us.

Some people tend to internalize their contempt while others tend to externalize it. People who are primarily Internalizers have problems with depression, caretaking, approval-seeking, lack of adequate boundaries, and lack of a sense of personal power. They have difficulty saying, "no" because that may bring disapproval, which is extremely anxiety-provoking since it is the opposite of what they seek. Persons that are predominantly Externalizers are less likely to be aware of their behavior and the effect it has on others. They believe other people should do things their way, tend to be self-centered, intrusive, have rigid boundaries, may have an excessive need to be right, and proclaim that they don't need anyone.

Externalizers have a tendency to demonstrate what Bradshaw calls *"shameless behavior."* Shameless behavior is seen in situations of abuse where the abuser is exercising god-like control over the victim. Examples of shameless behavior include sexual, physical, and emotional abuse. Shameless Externalizers develop a very thick scab. In the extreme cases, the person involved in shameless behavior is unaware on a conscious level that his behavior is wrong or sometimes even that it is hurtful to the victim. On an unconscious level, Externalizers cannot escape the reality of their behavior or its impact on the victim. The unconscious mind knows all; the shame, guilt, and remorse continue to accumulate for Externalizers, even though they are largely unaware of it. As their infection of shame grows, so does their contempt along with the need to externalize it. This build-up of contempt may eventually lead the Externalizer to episodes of the violent and/or dangerous behavior described earlier in this chapter.

The False Self

The wound of abandonment, the infection of shame, and the scab of contempt forms a free-floating mass of pain just beneath the surface of our awareness which creates in a child a false sense of identity – A False Self [see Fig. 5].

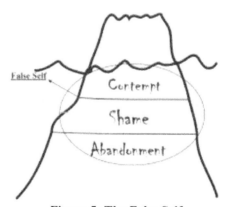

Figure 5: The False Self

The term "False Self" is used because it is just that–false, not true; a counterfeit self. It really feels like who we are, whether we were the child back there-and-then or the adult reading this book here-and-now. But this is not who we really are, and I hope to prove that in a moment. It *feels that way* because the wound is *emotional in nature*. Despite our best efforts, we cannot simply transfer the intellectual reality of this truth to our emotional reality. It is not until significant healing of the emotional wounds takes place that we are able to *feel* differently about ourselves.

Many times we have heard the saying, "kids are resilient." This is likely an effort to minimize our own guilt about not having been able to protect and/or nurture them the way they needed. While it is true that kids are resilient, the implication that they are now fine and have bounced back is not accurate. Emotional wounds do not go away. They must be tended to just like any other wound or the infection grows, and it gets worse. "Kids are survivors" is a more accurate statement. In the next chapter, we begin to explore how a child learns to survive and even get some of her needs met despite difficult circumstances. The skills they learn help them to survive, but they don't go very far in helping them effectively cope with adult life or have an intimate relationship.

Again, if you are a parent, please stay with your feelings about your own childhood experiences as much as possible as you read. Try to avoid getting lost in worry or guilt over your children. There is good news to come. For now, keep in mind that the best way to help them is to help *you* first. They learn by watching what you do, so demonstrate for them how to heal. Yes, get them into counseling if they need it and pay attention to their behavior if they are acting out. However, take care of yourself in the process too.

Chapter 3

The Art of Survival

In order for children to survive the pain of their wounds they must learn to live outside themselves; i.e., they must develop an *external focus* [see Fig. 6]. In other words, the child must find distractions in their outer world to avoid the pain of their inner world. Everything outside of our own skin is our outer world, while our thoughts and feelings exist only in our inner world. We experience our feelings in our body while our thoughts are located in our mind.

External Focus

Children develop this external focus through a number of distractions such as imaginary friends, relationships with pets or stuffed animals, watching cartoons, and staying busy with play. Later the distraction may be video games, skateboarding, or sports. Kids who have a lot of pain have difficulty with inactivity and quite time. One will often hear them proclaim, *"I'm bored! I can't stand boredom!"*

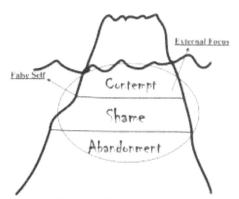

Figure 6: External Focus

In my work with teenagers, I encountered the "I can't stand boredom" syndrome many times before I learned that it really is true for some. Many kids have trouble tolerating boredom not because of boredom itself, but because of what boredom represents to them. Boredom to these wounded kids is a red flag. It's a signal that they are losing their external focus. As their attention begins to drift inward, anxiety starts to build because the next thing to come into their awareness would be their emotional pain. It rarely gets that far because the children or teenagers are compelled to take action to help them regain their external focus. A common scenario follows:

Billy, a teenager, is referred to counseling for habitually skipping school. Through the counseling process, it is discovered that this child's father is alcoholic and that things at home are fairly chaotic most of the time. In order to keep an external focus and avoid his emotional pain, Billy has to remain actively involved and interested in class. However, every day, right after lunch Billy has a math class. He is not interested in math at all because he is not very good at it (competence issue) so it is only a short time before "boredom" sets in.

Billy tries to regain his external focus by staring out the window in a daydream. That works for about three minutes. Soon, he finds himself passing notes, shooting spitballs, or talking to his neighbor. Before long, the teacher is involved in disciplining Billy, again, for disrupting the classroom. Billy then gets into an argument with his teacher, who is "always picking on me" (externalization of contempt). The teacher takes him out into the hall where the next external focus, the principal, is approaching.

Billy has the option of going through this routine or avoiding it altogether by skipping the class. The easiest option is to skip class and find some way to regain his external focus. Sometimes he would get a friend to sneak off with him to go to hangout downtown, or he would sneak off onto the parking lot to drink or do drugs, or simply go home to watch videos, play on the Internet, or engage in some other distraction.

Acting-out is only one method that helps children distract from their emotional pain. Again, other methods include creating imaginary friends, having relationships with stuffed animals or pets, video games, comic books, cartoons, hyperactivity, and various other ways to stay outside of themselves.

Invented Self

Another thing a child must do in order to avoid her inner world and stay in her outer world is to unconsciously build a wall between her awareness and her unawareness. These "walls" are constructed automatically of psychological defense mechanisms and have been collectively referred to as *"survival roles"* because their function is to help children survive in the face of unmet dependency needs. Children learn to "cover up" their false self by projecting an image other people might find acceptable. This is often referred to as "wearing a mask." I think of it as inventing a self [see Fig. 7] to cover up the false self because, "If people really knew me they would not like me (shame), and they would reject me (fear of more abandonment)."

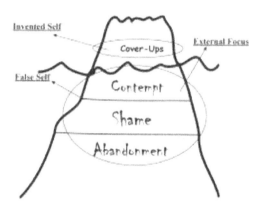

Figure 7: Invented Self

Children unwittingly invent and project these images, or survival roles, through the use of unconscious defense mechanisms in order to avoid the intolerable reality of their unmet needs. The pain is still there, but it is not as "in their face" as it would be due to one defense known as repression. Repression automatically pushes the pain deep into their subconscious until the child matures, and heals, enough to develop the psychological equipment to cope with it.

Survival roles also serve to help the child find ways to get her needs for time, attention, affection, and direction met. For example, in a dysfunctional family one parent gets caught up in some form of problematic behavior while the other gets caught up with trying to control or "fix" the problem parent. They get enmeshed with each other and the problem behavior while leaving less and less time to attend to anything else, including the children.

Family Hero:

When the first child comes along, he or she finds out fairly quickly that in order to get any time, attention, affection, and direction in this family he or she has to do something outstanding to get noticed. So this child usually becomes the *Hero*. There are two kinds of family heroes. The first is the flashy hero who gets all A's, is captain of the football team, valedictorian, class president, head cheerleader or a combination of the above. The second type is the behind-the-scenes hero; aka the *Responsible One* or the *Parentified Child*. This is the child who comes home from school early every day, does the laundry, gets the mail, prepares dinner, does the dishes, takes care of the younger kids and, in essence, becomes a parent at ten years old.

Rebel/Scapegoat:

The second child usually becomes the *Rebel* or *Scapegoat*. They can rarely compete with the first child for the positive attention because the Hero has a head start. So the Rebel must settle for the next-best thing, i.e., negative attention. The Rebel gets time, attention, affection, and direction from teachers, principals, juvenile officers, counselors and anyone else who would try to help them. While they may not get the positive attention, they do end up getting the most attention. The parents must stop what they are doing to deal with this kid's misbehavior because the school or juvenile office keeps calling.

Lost Child:

The third child cannot compete for the positive attention or the negative attention, so they don't get any attention and become the *Lost Child*. In order to survive, this child relies on fantasy to get her needs partially met. An example of a Lost Child is the seven-year-old girl who is always somewhere in the background playing with a doll that she has had forever. One hardly ever notices that she is even there. She says nice things to the doll, combs its hair, tucks her in every night, rocks her to sleep and, in essence, creates a family of her own, vicariously getting her needs met by becoming a nurturing parent to the doll. The Lost Child may also have anywhere from eight to twelve stuffed animals on her bed at one time and knows each of them intimately. This child spends so much time in her fantasy world that she loses out on opportunities to make friends in the real world.

Family Mascot:

The fourth child, usually the *Mascot*, is the baby of the family. This child gets his needs met through being on stage. He or she is the class clown or the beauty queen. This child's job is to bring entertainment to the family, usually in the form of humor.

The roles described above are the classic survival roles described by Sharon Wegscheider-Cruse (1991) in her book *The Family Trap*. These roles do not always follow the pattern described above, but considerably more often than not, they do. The firstborn is usually the Hero because it is the preferred role, and the child has the first crack at it. All kids want the positive attention and honor assigned to the Hero. However, if that mask is taken, then the next children have to settle for the next-best thing. The Rebel is the second most effective role. Even though the attention is negative, they get lots more of it because the parents have to deal with this child's misbehavior, so the Rebel becomes the priority. Middle children are more like to get lost in the crowd, so they must sharpen their skills with fantasy in order to survive. These children also tend to be chameleons, switching from one survival role to another whenever the opportunity presents itself. Many times they experience all the roles in their life at one time or another. The baby of the family is almost always the center of attention so it is not surprising that these children make the most of that and become the Mascot.

So, it is *birth order, not personality, not willfulness, and not inherently bad character* that reinforces or "shapes" the original masks we learn to wear. Children do not decide to behave this way, they instinctively act-out these roles until they find the one that works the best in getting them the time, attention, affection and direction they need. Heroes get it from teachers, coaches, newspaper reporters, and others who are amazed by their outstanding abilities. Rebels gets it from teachers, principals, juvenile officers, counselors, and anyone else who wants to help them get back on track. The Lost Child gets it through fantasy, and the Mascot gets it through being on stage.

These roles are also reinforced at home because they all bring something to the family, helping the system to survive as well. The Hero brings honor to the family. The Rebel brings distraction, which takes the focus off the primary dysfunction in the marital pair. This is why another term used for the Rebel is "Scapegoat." They act as a lightning rod help to keep the family intact because, if the parents have too much time to face what is going on between them, they might get a divorce, and the family then disintegrates. The Lost Child brings relief because you never have to worry about this child and hardly notice he is there. The Mascot brings entertainment and humor, diffusing the seriousness of the family dysfunction. All of these roles look different on the outside, but they are all alike on the inside.

Impression Management

Another function of the Invented Self is to manage the impressions of others that are important to us. Impression Management is driven by the "what-would-other-people-think" syndrome. It goes something like this: If I have ten people in my life who are important to me, and one of them is not happy with me while the other nine think I am the greatest thing in the world, I would focus much of my energy thinking about how I could get that one back in line with the others. If two or three get upset with me, I get anxious. If four or five of them don't think much of me, I get disparate or panicky because it almost feels like I am dying.

It feels like I am dying because, in a way, I am. I draw my identity, my sense of self, from those ten people. Hence, I must be vigilant in managing the impressions of those around me. If they accept me and think I am okay then I must be ... right? Not necessarily—even if they accept me—I cannot truly accept their acceptance because, at another level, I feel like a phony. An example of this is when we have difficulty accepting compliments from others. Somewhere inside the voice of shame is telling us *"They wouldn't say that if they really knew you!"* The voice may even be inaudible, but we feel like a phony anyway. This accounts for the paradox of why we tend to discount or minimize anything positive coming from those we try to please.

The survival roles described above are examples of the masks we learn to wear in childhood. As we grow and the pain continues to accumulate, we get more and more sophisticated in the masks we wear. For a fairly complete catalog of masks read John Powell's book (1995) *Why I am afraid to tell you who I am.*

Chapter 4

Who Am I Really?

As we have seen, the *False Self* is just that–false. It is an emotional wound and, like any other wound, it has gotten infected due to lack of attention. The severity of the wound of abandonment and the infection of shame are hard to see because they are covered by the scab of contempt, and for the most part, it is out of our awareness. We have also seen that our *Invented Self* is not who we are either. The False Self poses as our private self and the Invented Self as our public self, but both are imposters or counterfeits–so who are we really? For anyone who has ever struggled with addiction, codependency, and/or dysfunctional relationships, that is the million-dollar question.

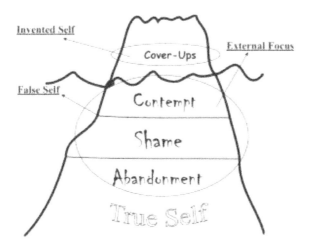

Figure 8: True Self

I mentioned in Chapter 2 that I think I can prove to the reader that the False Self is not who we really are. I know I can prove it to some, and I think I can prove it to others, but I am not sure I can prove it to all. Here goes: If you believe there is a Divine Creator, do you think He would want a small child to feel defective at her very core? Would a loving God want children to go through their entire childhood feeling rotten through and through? That everything bad that happens is their fault? Of course not!

This is proof *for believers* that the False Self is *not* what God created. No, these emotional wounds *are what life created*. The *True Self* is what God created, and it has been with us in our inner world since before we were born. Then life happened. The wounds grew and covered up the True Self, pushing it far beneath the surface of our awareness before we even had a chance to get to know ourselves. It was replaced with an imposter; as a child we bought it and learned to live outside ourselves, abandoning our inner world. Then we poured a slab of concrete over it (Invented Self), locking it all in place and effectively alienating ourselves from who we were created to be [Fig. 8].

It is my belief that the True Self is who God created and that this is where our spirit resides. I also believe this is why God feels especially far away to some. Our spirit is what connects with his Spirit. To the extent that we don't have access to our spirit, we feel cut-off from God. Our True Self is also where our purpose resides. In Rick Warren's book, *A Purpose-Driven Life* (2002, 2007), the author points out that our purpose is not really *our* purpose at all ... it is *His* purpose for us. We were created with a special set of talents and abilities in order to perform His purpose for us.

In the Bible, it says that *"He who overcomes himself is greater than he who overcomes a city."* Do you wonder which "self" we are to overcome? In another place, the Bible says, *"Blessed are those who mourn: for they shall be comforted."* Is *refusing to mourn* not what we do when we wear a mask, ignore our inner world, and pretend that everything is fine? When God feels far away, could it be because our True Self, the part of us that connects with him, is buried so deep under the wounds of the False Self that we cannot feel his presence? If the answers to these questions are "yes," then turning our focus inward to surface and grieve our pain is the royal road to *true comfort and relief*. As we shall see in the next chapter, seeking comfort and relief in all the wrong places inevitably leads to more pain.

Even if you are agnostic, or atheist, for that matter, I think most can believe in the innocence of a child. We all come into this world innocent and pure. That innocent, pure True Self gets wounded and covered up by this world regardless of your religious or spiritual beliefs. For those of you who believe neither in God, nor in the inherent goodness of man, I may not have been able to provide sufficient proof of the True Self. If not, I challenge you to look within and see if it might be contempt and emotional wounds that are getting in your way. I believe in you and wish you all the wonderful things that life has to offer.

The next logical questions are, *"How do we deal with this? How do we uncover our True Self?"* The good news is that there are answers to these questions. The bad news is that we first have more pain and consequences of emotional trauma to explore before we can answer them.

Chapter 5

Illusions of Comfort and Relief

Pain as a Motivator

As already pointed out, the role of pain in our life is to motivate us to do something different. Pain lets us know that what we are doing is not working by signaling that we are moving further away from happiness. It is a warning system that tells us when something is wrong or when something needs attention. Remember the formula from Chapter 1, A → B? This formula is not rocket science so why do we keep doing the same things over and over expecting a different outcome each time? The easiest answer to that question is *because we don't know what else to do*. We are all doing our best to achieve that one ultimate goal in life, to be happy. Perhaps happiness eludes us due to the progressively dysfunctional methods we unwittingly rely upon to feel better. Soon the best we can hope for is comfort and relief.

We don't like pain and when we encounter it, we are compelled to seek comfort and relief. Growing up with all of this woundedness is painful. So where do we find comfort and relief? We cannot generate any good feelings on the inside because we can't even go there, it is too painful. So, we must look to things outside of us for comfort and relief. Since we are all genetically and psychologically "wired" a little differently, we will find one or two things that "really does it" for us. Some of us are wired for alcohol or other drugs, others for excessive working, spending, drama, risk-taking, sexing, gambling, eating, and others for addictive relationships. These are only a few of the distractions available to us in this candy store we call America. [Fig. 9]

Emotional Attachments

When we find the object or event that "really does it for us" then we attach to it on an emotional level because *we love what it does for us*. It provides us with a very powerful, instantaneous, although short-lived feeling. Soon *we begin to trust the object or event* because it does what it is supposed to do (make us feel better) very quickly, very powerfully; in a way no one and nothing else can– every single time we ask it to. So, we attach to the object or event on an emotional level.

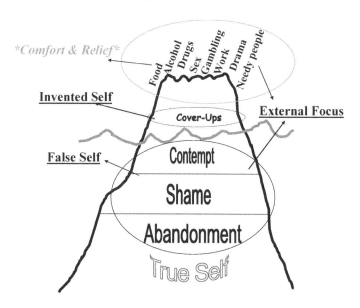

Figure 10: Comfort and Relief

Love and trust are the main ingredients for a primary relationship. This emotional attachment signals the beginning of a serious problem because we are not supposed to have primary relationships with objects and events. Our primary relationships are supposed to be with people who are important to us. Craig Nakken defines addiction in his book, *The Addictive Personality*. According to Nakken, addiction is, "a pathological relationship with an object or event that produces a desired mood swing." This is, in my opinion, the best definition of addiction I have heard. I do, however, take the liberty of making one minor distinction for the benefit of my clients. I define addiction as *"an unhealthy primary relationship with an object or event that produces a desired mood swing."* I make this distinction for a couple of reasons. First of all, "pathological" seems to produce more stigma than "unhealthy" even though they mean the same thing. Secondly, "primary" highlights why the relationship is unhealthy.

Most people don't realize and will, in fact, initially deny that they have such a strong emotional attachment to their addiction of choice. In both treatment groups and individual sessions, I have asked my addicted clients the following question for the past several years, always with the same results: *"What is the most important relationship in your life?"* They will respond with *"My wife, my kids, my mom, my boyfriend or girlfriend."* I always just shake my head and say *"Wrong answer."* They initially get a little indignant that I would be so presumptuous to assume I know what is more important to them than they do themselves. Then all I have to say is *"When was the last time you lied to your mom about ..., broke a promise to your kids about ..., broke up with a girlfriend over... etc."* There is rarely an argument. I close this discussion with *"Maybe in your heart, they are most important to you, but in your life the reality is that the addiction trumps everything else."*

Let's look for a moment at the implications of this emotional attachment to an object or event. First of all, the question of "choice" frequently comes up. For example, "He chose to start; he can choose to stop!" This attachment is a love and trust relationship just like any other love and trust relationship. When was the last time you "chose" to fall in love with someone? How easy is it to end a relationship with someone you love, even when you know it is for the best? When you do end such a relationship you can expect to grieve. Since this is one of the most important relationships in your life the grief process kicks in full-steam when one decides to get help and give up their addiction. This is manageable if we have the internal coping skills and external support network to manage the pain of this "letting-go" process. However, if we have this unhealthy primary relationship in the first place that implies that we have neither the skills nor the support necessary to manage the pain associated with this loss. So we fall back on the object or activity that we trust the most. This is precisely why people relapse into their addiction and precisely how they eventually lose their "choice" to "just quit." To make matters worse, in some cases, there is the physical pain of withdrawal to contend with as well.

The comfort we achieve through this relationship with an object or event is an illusion. Remember, the wounds we must relieve in order to be happy is *emotional in nature*. Therefore, we need emotional comfort and relief, such as the kind we get when our basic needs are met, in order to heal and be healthy. The "comfort and relief" we achieve through the use of our object or event of choice is not emotional but physiological or *physical in nature*. In other words, we learn to mask our emotional pain with "medicine." That means any time we have a feeling we don't like, we medicate it rather than listen to it, understand it, and respond to it. This just pushes the feeling back down inside to accumulate with the pain that is already there. Using a chemical to medicate our emotional pain is tantamount to masking a serious back injury with painkillers while we go on working. We keep doing more and more damage without realizing it because our "warning system" (pain) was taken out of the way. Thus we continue to do things to increase our shame, guilt, contempt, and remorse. We prove it over and over again, that "we can't do anything right". We eventually abandon our money, our families, our cars, our pride, our careers, our dreams, our goals, ourselves, etc. As our pain increases, so does our need for "comfort and relief" [Fig. 10].

Sooner or later we will crash and "hit bottom" [Fig. 11]. This happens when we have accumulated so much pain that there is not enough "comfort and relief" to offset it anymore. The "coping skill" that used to work instantly now only barely works. This is when we are using just to feel normal. Some addictions get us there faster than others. Some addictions are too easy to hide. For instance, if we are addicted to alcohol, we can get a DWI or DUI, but if we have an addiction to work, we get a bonus.

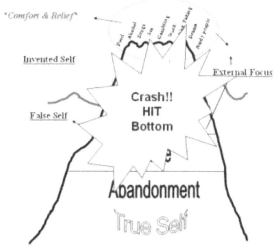

Figure 11: Hitting Bottom

Hitting Bottom

A major obstacle to hitting bottom are the well-intentioned others who enable us by interfering with the A → B formula mentioned earlier. People who love and care about us want to help when we are in trouble. For example, when we do "A" (spend our rent money on alcohol) we should receive "B" (have to deal with it ourselves–i.e., take on extra work to pay the rent or be evicted). However, when someone steps in and gives us "C" (pays our rent for us "this time") instead of letting us experience "B" then they have become our enabler. "Enablers" helps maintain our addiction a little longer by reducing or eliminating our pain. Remember pain is a motivator and teacher. "Tough Love" means stepping out of the way and letting us experience "B." Often times our chief enabler is just as wounded as we are, so we have become their external focus. Think about it, what better way to distract from our own problems than to find a "problem person" to focus on. We tend to choose people on an unconscious as well as a conscious level. This explains how many people end up getting out of one bad relationship only to find that they are right back in another. Such people have an excessive need to be needed. They are Internalizers who find comfort and relief from becoming important to others. You will often hear other people say about them, *"What a saint of a woman! Look at all she goes through, and still she sticks with him!"* The masks they wear include the Martyr, The Rescuer, and the Victim.

Until we do get our wake-up call, unconscious psychological defenses block acceptance of the reality and extent of our addiction. Examples are: *Rationalization* (Excuse making, justifying); *Projection* (Blaming anything and anyone except the real problem); *Minimizing* (It's not that bad, I can quit anytime I want); *Diversion Tactics* (debating, arguing, withdrawing, and changing the subject); *Disarming* (That's just the way I am), *Hostility* (Intimidating others who try to talk about it); etc.

When the "call" does come, we are likely to reach out for help. The irony of this is that many people who reach out for help with their pain don't really want to know what's bothering them because their denial is still intact. They just know they want comfort and relief. For those readers who need help, I hope that this book will raise your bottom to the point you get it sooner than later. Unfortunately, some have a very high tolerance for pain, and they wait too long and some tragedy strikes. You don't have to wait until that happens. It is not easy, but with honesty, open-mindedness, and willingness you can recover!

Chapter 6

The Twilight Zone

Recovery from addiction is easy–*all you have to do is change your whole life*.

The transition from the old life to the new is a period of limbo where the past is too painful to return to and the future is too uncertain to feel comfortable about. There is much to be done, and it cannot be done all at once. If one plunges headlong into their emotional pain, they will be compelled to seek comfort and relief in the only way they know how which results in a relapse into their addiction of choice. The first thing one must do is give up their comfort and relief [Fig. 12], accept that they cannot recover alone, and reach out to others for help. For these reasons, the *pain of not reaching out* for help must outweigh the *pain of continuing to engage* in the addiction.

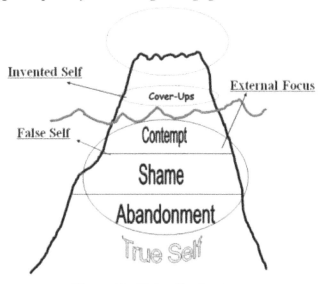

Figure 12: Giving Up Comfort

Reaching Out

Reaching out to others is an interpersonal skill that we are not born with. *Acting out* is the instinct children are born with in order to express their needs. If we grew up with a significant amount of emotional pain then we are not likely to be very good at reaching out because it was either not taught or not allowed. Furthermore, the infection of shame makes it very difficult to ask for help. Often, it is only when the pain grows to an unbearable proportion that we begin to consider reaching out. Adding the accumulated shame of our entire life with having to admit a problem with alcohol, drugs, sex, food, or gambling, to name a few, gives us an idea of the magnitude of the problem one can have with asking for help. Can you hear the voice of shame? *"See, now you are really proving what a loser you are!"*

Reaching out requires a certain amount of self-disclosure, i.e. taking off the mask of the Invented-Self. The need to manage the impressions of others cries out to keep quiet and find some other way to work this out. This is the primary reason that such value is placed upon the anonymity of members of 12-Step groups. They realize the importance of safety to those newcomers who may be considering reaching out by attending a meeting for the first time. Even when the pain is great enough to bring someone in for counseling, they are compelled to manage the impression of the counselor to the extent that it can actually sabotage the assessment process. Here the person who has "reached out" by making the counseling appointment will answer many of the questions in a way that suggests they are fine and there really is no problem. Sometimes it takes a few sessions before they begin to feel safe enough with the helper, the environment, and the confidentiality to open up.

Internalizers are a little more likely to reach out early than Externalizers because the latter has an excessive need to be right. Externalizers are "shameless" because their defenses are geared toward making everyone else responsible for their problems. To admit a problem of any kind requires taking an inward look. This is highly irregular for an Externalizer because their shamelessness is in proportion to the actual shame and pain they would feel if they could see the truth. So, again, the pain of hitting bottom must outweigh the pain of facing their inner world before they are motivated to reach out.

On the other hand, the defenses of Internalizers are geared toward self-contempt. They are "not important, never right about anything, total failures, and unworthy of happiness." These are the very depressing thoughts of an Internalizer which make them already depressed even before the wake-up call comes. Again, most people are rarely at one end of the contempt continuum or the other, although there are some cases in which this is true. More often, we have a tendency to slide up and down on that line internalizing for as long as we can stand it then blowing up occasionally to externalize, or dump, some of that contempt.

When people do feel enough pain to come in for help many times their denial is still largely intact. They may say, "I am here to get help with my depression." The therapist might ask, "Why are you depressed?" Client: "I don't know." Therapist: "Well, do you drink?" Client: "Yes, but that's not my concern right now." Therapist: "How much and how often do you drink?" Client, "Probably too much, I have had three DUI's, but that's not why I am here. I came because I am depressed." Therapist: "If that is not the problem then do you have any theories about what is?" Client, "You're the therapist, you tell me!"

This person is still looking for ways to avoid giving up his unhealthy primary relationship with alcohol. He wants help to find comfort and relief but is still fighting that painful inward look. He is already in pain and to let go of his denial too soon might be overwhelming. Care must be taken to go forward at an acceptable pace building coping skills and supports first. If one is to give up their primary coping skill, they must have something to replace it with prior to doing to work ahead. Even then, it gets worse before it gets better.

People who reach out later than sooner are usually so full of shame that when they do take that initial inward look, they say things like, *"Man, I don't even have any values anymore!"* I had one person tell me they felt that they had actually become evil. In addition to the toxic shame, what they have become emotionally infected with is the normal guilt and remorse they feel for the bad things they have done during their addiction.

The food addict is full of shame over repeated failures to control their eating. The sex addict is full of shame over the inability to honor the marriage by staying faithful. The gambling addict is full of shame over the inability to take care of his family due to overwhelming debt. The work-a-holic is full of shame over hundreds of broken promises to spend time with his wife and kids.

Recovery – A Hard Sell

Imagine you are reaching out for help because you are in the most emotional pain you have ever felt. Now imagine hearing the helper say that you need to give up the only comfort and relief you've ever known and face this pain [Fig. 12]. That's what it is like for someone who finds themselves at the bottom. It is a very hard sell even when the person knows you are right. Along with reaching out, abstinence is another of the first things we need to accomplish if we are going to heal.

At this point, some simple definitions are in order. *Abstinence* means not engaging in *any* unhealthy relationships with objects or events to produce a desired mood swing. Many times people give up their addiction of choice only to begin relying on another unhealthy relationship to medicate their pain. Alcoholics may switch to marijuana; sex addicts may switch to gambling, gambling addicts to drinking, compulsive spenders to food, etc. This is called *substitution* because we are simply substituting *one unhealthy relationship for another*. It's like a rebound relationship; how long are we likely to stay with our second choice when we know our first choice is waiting in the wings? This is a strategy many people employ even before they get to the point of needing to reach out. It doesn't work because it only addresses the need for comfort and relief. The rest of The Iceberg remains intact. Sooner or later the emotional pain flares up again and the substitute just doesn't get it. *Cross-addiction* is what happens when the substitute *does do just as much* for us as the unhealthy relationship of choice. But now we have two addictions to overcome because the new one almost always leads back to the old one.

Abstinence is a required task in order for recovery to take place. How does one abstain from food addictions, sex addiction, work addictions, and spending addictions? Abstinence in these cases means using the objects and events only in the healthy ways for which they are intended. This means we eat for the right reasons, we have sex for the right reasons with the right person, we balance work with the other areas of our lives, and we spend for the right reasons. We avoid self-medicating while improving emotional coping skills, building a support network, learning how to communicate, and healing the internal wounds.

Prescription for Recovery

Recovery means abstaining and liking it better than engaging in unhealthy relationships with objects or events. The only way we are going to like abstinence better than engaging in our addictions is when we find comfort from the internal healing that begins to take place. This healing can only occur through the development of healthy recovery-oriented behaviors and activities.

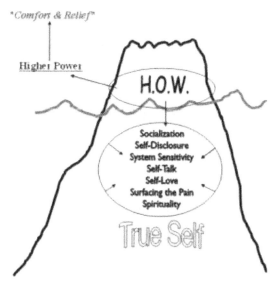

Figure 13: Turing Focus Inward

In the 12-Step groups, suggested recovery activities are:
- Go to Recovery Meetings
- Get a Sponsor
- Pray and Meditate
- Read Recovery Literature
- Practice the 12 Steps of Recovery

In his Video, *Shame and Addiction* John Bradshaw suggests:

Socialization – Attend non-shaming recovery or church groups
- Self-Disclosure – Come out of hiding, break the no-talk rule
- System Sensitivity – Understand the family system you came from
- Self-Talk – Positive affirmations
- Self-Love – Take care of yourself
- Surfacing the Pain – Talk about it, understand it, get it out
- Spirituality – Prayer and Meditation

Relapse means undoing recovery enough to be able to return to an unhealthy relationship. Relapse is a process that ends when we re-engage our addictive relationship of choice. One cannot relapse without a period of recovery. A period of abstinence with no recovery activities is called stopping. "Stopping" is easy; staying stopped is the hard part. Stopping is always followed by starting again. This is why a good friend of mine in recovery likes to say, *"I can't stop drinking because if I stop, I know I will start again."* He reminds himself and others, "I can abstain one day at a time by the grace of a power greater than myself."

What Next?

As mentioned throughout this book, arresting addictions, codependency, chronic depression, and other long-term life problems is a critical piece, but it is only the *"tip of the Iceberg."* Stabilizing these conditions through the development of healthy coping skills and a good support network is the foundation for the work that lies ahead. Many people recover through the use of the 12-Step programs and other community support programs alone. Some people speed the healing process up with the inclusion of therapy as part of their recovery program.

However, what about that one ultimate goal that we all have in common—that state of being that we all pursue so vigorously? I have found that happiness–i.e., *contentment, fulfillment, satisfaction, wholeness and completeness,* is not something we can seek and find. It is a byproduct of living the way we were intended to live—as our True Self [Fig. 14]. Codependency, chronic depression, Adult/Child Syndrome, and the many other long-term consequences of abandonment, shame and contempt are OPTIONAL. You don't have to live that way anymore. If you feel ready now, begin working on Part I of the *Thawing the Iceberg* recovery program in the following pages.

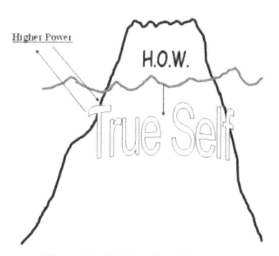

Figure 14: Finding Your True Self

Thawing
Adult/Child Syndrome

The Workbook

Section 1: Getting to know your "False Self"

1.1 The Wound of Abandonment

Unmet childhood dependency needs cause emotional wounds to develop in a child. By "dependency" needs, we mean those critical needs children cannot get met on their own. They depend on their parents to meet these needs. If children get these needs met on a consistent and regular basis they thrive and flourish. If they do not get these needs met, they suffer. There are two groups of dependency needs:

Group One - Survival Needs:
- Food
- Shelter
- Clothing
- Medical Attention
- Safety and Protection

The first four survival needs are a given, but the last one warrants some discussion. Children must feel safe and protected in order to grow and develop. Children learn through play. They cannot play, unless they can relax. If they don't feel safe then they must always be on guard, scanning their environment for signs of danger. This hyper-vigilance tends to keep their anxiety level too high to relax enough for play.

In order to feel safe all children go through a psychological process called *Idealization*. This is where they idealize their parents seeing them as omnipotent (all powerful) and omniscient (all knowing) god-like creatures. It goes something like this, "If god-like creatures protect me then nothing can get to me." (We will come back to this term in the next section on Shame.)

Exercise - Children who do not get their survival needs met have experienced trauma of some sort. Below are several types of trauma-producing experiences and events. *Check the ones that apply to you and your childhood experiences.*

- ☐ Sexual abuse
- ☐ Physical abuse
- ☐ Emotional abuse or neglect: Emotionally unavailable parent(s) or parents who give their child the opposite of what they need such as name-calling, belittling, threats of abandonment, shaming, etc.
- ☐ Psychological abuse: Ignoring the child as if they do not exist, denial of a child's reality such as telling them they didn't see what they saw (e.g., "Daddy wasn't drunk, don't you ever say that again!")
- ☐ Frequent Moves
- ☐ Prolonged separation from a parent
- ☐ Reversal of parent/child roles
- ☐ Rigid family rules
- ☐ Divorce
- ☐ Death of a parent or other family member
- ☐ Mentally Ill parent or family member
- ☐ Cruel and Unusual punishment: such as locking a child in the closet
- ☐ Other trauma producing behaviors:
  - ☐ Humiliating
  - ☐ Degrading
  - ☐ Inflicting Guilt
  - ☐ Criticizing
  - ☐ Disgracing
  - ☐ Joking about
  - ☐ Laughing at
  - ☐ Teasing
  - ☐ Manipulating
  - ☐ Deceiving
  - ☐ Tricking
  - ☐ Betraying
  - ☐ Hurting

- ☐ Being Cruel
- ☐ Belittling
- ☐ Intimidating
- ☐ Patronizing
- ☐ Threatening
- ☐ Inflicting Fear
- ☐ Discounting
- ☐ Reversing Roles
- ☐ Don't Talk
- ☐ Don't Feel
- ☐ Don't Trust
- ☐ Rigid Boundaries
- ☐ No Boundaries
- ☐ Controlling
- ☐ Withdrawing/Withholding Love
- ☐ Discrediting
- ☐ Invalidating
- ☐ Misleading
- ☐ Breaking Promises
- ☐ Chaotic Environment
- ☐ Cold, Uncaring
- ☐ Environment
- ☐ Making Unclear Demands
- ☐ Disapproving
- ☐ Ignoring
- ☐ Denying Reality

Describe those you have experienced in your life and how you felt about them at the time and how you feel about them now as you write:

_____

_____

_____

_____

_____

_____

_____

_____
_____
_____
_____
_____
_____
_____
_____

Group Two – Emotional Needs:
- Time
- Attention
- Affection
- Direction

These are the needs that nurture the child. It's like we have an emotional gas tank. When we get these needs met fully we feel full, content, satisfied, etc. When we do not get these needs met at all we feel an ache, a longing, a great emptiness that won't go away. Perhaps we get these needs met half the time, so we feel half-full but still feel an ache, as if something is missing.

Time: Children get it that whatever their parents give their time to is what they love. Each child must receive enough quality time with each parent to get the message that they are loved and just as important as anyone else in the family. "Quality time" is time that includes getting the other needs met.

Attention: We "attend" to children not just by listening, but also by understanding, validating their feelings, noticing when they are struggling, helping them figure out what they feel, showing genuine concern and curiosity about who they are, what they are doing, how their day went, etc.

Affection: Hugs, kisses, pats on the back, bragging about them while they are in earshot, words of encouragement, etc.

Most of all children need an affectionate climate in the home. We need the "affection thermostat" in the home to be turned up toward warm and cozy, rather than cold and distant. Affection sends the message to kids that we approve of them, that we like who they are and who they are becoming, that we like being their parent.

Direction: Kids need two forms of direction:

- ***Guidance***: "Here is how we do anger, here's how we behave in public, here's how we get along …" Parents must be available and approachable. Helping kids learn how to do things is critical to building their sense of competence and mastery.

For example, teaching a child to ride a bike requires us to hold onto the bike until we feel they are ready to try it on their own. We know they are likely to fall and may get injured, but we let them go anyway. Soon the child is "doing it." They even say, "Look! I'm doing it!" This is a statement of competence and evidence that their ego has just received a big boost.

Overprotection or "over-doing" for the child can also hurt a child's sense of competence. Sometimes parents cannot bear the thought of what could happen if the child crashes so they never let go of the bike. Not only does the child miss the "I'm doing it!" experience, but also they get a message from the god-like creature in their life that they probably can't do it. So they get a message of incompetence.

- ***Discipline***: Healthy limits are not harsh, abusive, or inconsistent. They are firm, effective, and consistent. Kids need someone to provide limits in their life, or they don't feel safe. They need to know someone is going to be there to tell them where the line is.

Unmet dependency needs results in wounded children. These wounds do not heal if they are left unattended. In fact, ignored wounds get "infected" as we will see later. There are of course many other human needs to consider as well …

Exercise - Explore the following questions in as much detail as you can. Focus especially on how your needs got met, *or didn't get met* in these relationships–*rather than saying "good" or "bad" say exactly how it was good or bad, and then look at the needs above to describe how it could have been better.* Use the margins of the paper or add sheets where necessary. (You get out of this as much as you put into it.):

Describe your relationship with your father as specifically as possible especially as it relates to the two groups of Dependency needs outlined above:

_____

_____

_____

_____

_____

_____

_____

_____

_____

_____

_____

_____

_____

_____

_____

Describe your relationship with your mother as specifically as possible especially as it relates to the two groups of Dependency needs outlined above:

_____

_____

_____

_____

_____

_____

_____

_____

_____

_____

_____

_____

_____

_____

Describe your father's relationships with your mother–
especially how they did the "Mom/Dad" relationship and how
they did the "Husband/Wife" relationship:

_____

_____

_____

_____

_____

_____

_____

_____

_____

_____

_____

_____

_____

_____

_____

_____

_____

_____

Describe each of your parent's relationships with each of your
siblings in terms of the dependency needs outlined above. Did

they favor one over another? What roles did they assign to each of your siblings? (Hero, Rebel, Lost Child, Mascot, etc.)

_____

_____

_____

_____

_____

_____

_____

_____

_____

_____

_____

_____

_____

_____

_____

_____

Describe your relationship(s) with each of your siblings:

_____

_____

_____

_____

_____

_____

_____

_____

_____

_____

_____

_____

_____

_____

_____

_____

_____

_____
_____
_____

Describe your relationships with others at school and in your neighborhood:

_____
_____
_____
_____
_____
_____
_____
_____
_____
_____
_____
_____
_____
_____
_____
_____

1.2 The Infection of Shame

In the section above on abandonment we discussed the process of Idealization of the parents. If a child does not get their needs met, they suffer abandonment of those needs. The child cannot say, *"Well, Dad has alcoholism. I don't have to take it personal. He doesn't mean to break his promises. That's just part of the disease."*

Because of idealization children can take it no other way than personal. "God-like" creatures don't make mistakes because they are perfect. Children have no one else to blame for not getting their needs met than themselves. They begin to develop a sense of defectiveness or what John Bradshaw calls Toxic Shame.

Internal messages coming from that shame may sound like this:
- I'm not good enough
- I'm stupid
- I'm lazy
- I can't do anything right
- I'm ugly
- If I was a better kid mom and dad wouldn't fight so much
- How could anyone like me?
- Others?_____

If abandonment is the *original wound,* then shame is an *emotional infection* that sets it. The infection gets worse as the child grows, especially in shame-based family systems. A shame-based family system is one where messages of shame are delivered to its members daily.

We may hear things like:
- What's wrong with you?
- Why don't you know how to do that?

- I might as well do it myself!
- Why can't you be more like your brother?
- Why do you do this to me?
- If it weren't for you, I wouldn't have these headaches.
- Can't you do anything right?
- You are just like your father!
- I wish you'd never been born!
- You are going to end up in jail one of these days!
- Others?_____

In shame-based families we also have several unspoken or unwritten rules:

- Don't Talk: Don't talk about family business; don't talk about the drinking, etc.

- Don't Feel: It's not okay to have feelings, "You shouldn't feel that way!"

- Don't Think: It's not okay to have your own opinions and thoughts.

- Don't Trust: Don't trust people because they will always let you down.

Below are several other shame-based rules and messages in less-than-nurturing families–also known as *Injunctions & Counter-Injunctions*. We will explore these later when we get into uncovering your "Life Script." Check off those that you relate to most:

Shame-based Rules:

Don't express your feelings
Don't get angry
Don't feel that, feel this…
Don't cry
Do as I say, not as I do
Be Perfect
Avoid conflict (or avoid dealing with conflict)
Don't think or talk; just follow directions
Don't trust others
Don't betray the family
Don't discuss the family with outsiders; keep the family secret
Be seen and not heard!
No backtalk
Please Me!
Please Others
Don't think that, think this…
Always be in control
Be Strong!
Try Hard!
Don't question; Just do what you're told
Take care of others
Don't Be Close to Others
Don't ask for what you need

Shame-based Messages:

I wish I had never had you
Your needs don't matter
Hurry up!
What's wrong with you!?
Big boys don't cry
Act like a nice girl (or a lady)
You don't feel that way
We wanted a boy/girl
You're no good!
You are going to end up…(somewhere bad)
Of course we love you!
I'm sacrificing myself for you
How can you do this to me, after all I've done?
We won't love you if...
You're driving me crazy!
You'll never accomplish anything
That didn't hurt, crybaby!
You are so selfish!
You'll be the death of me yet!
That's not true...
I promise (then breaks it)
You make me sick!
You're stupid!
Others? _____

Exercise - Explore the following questions in as much detail as you can. You may have trouble putting these messages into words. That is because, as we will see in the material on Script Messages & Injunctions, some of these rule and messages were delivered in the pre-verbal years–before the ability to use or understand words–so they become inner pressure without words also known as Injunctions.

These rules and messages become the foundations for your Life Script. You can always add to these answers later. Use additional paper if necessary.

Discuss the unspoken shame-based rules and messages you grew up with. Do you still follow these rules today? How? Do you still hear the echo of the shame-based messages in your head? Be as specific as you can.

_____

_____

_____

_____

_____

_____

_____

_____

_____

_____

_____

_____

_____

_____

_____

_____

_____

If you feel you came from a shame-based family system describe what it was like and as much as you can about what happened. Give examples of shaming messages you heard whether they we directly spoken or non-spoken/implied messages:

_____
_____
_____
_____
_____
_____
_____
_____
_____
_____
_____
_____
_____

It is typical to internalize these rules and messages as children. They become embedded in the unconscious mind and may be experienced as mental "tapes" or recordings that just seem to play all on their own. Describe some of the internal rules and messages (self-talk) you experienced as a child:

_____
_____
_____
_____
_____
_____
_____
_____
_____

Describe the shaming self-talk you still experience today as an adult:

_____

_____

_____

_____

_____

_____

_____

_____

Describe the thoughts and feelings you have about your ability to do things such as asking for help, applying for a new job, asking for a raise, joining a new group, going out in public, etc.

_____

_____

_____

_____

_____

_____

_____

_____

Sometimes, through a complex psychological maneuver, we overcompensate for shame by convincing ourselves we are need-*less*, *"I don't need anything from anyone."* We learn how not to care anymore. Write as much as you can about this if applicable to you.

_____

_____

_____

_____

_____

_____

_____

_____

Other times we feel overwhelmed by shame to the point that we feel helpless, inadequate and needy. Sometimes it may even feel as though we are needy children again. Describe as much as you can about this if applicable to you.

_____

_____

_____

_____

_____

_____

_____

_____

Toxic shame can be poisoning our emotional life, to the extent that we are subject to "shame attacks" at any given moment. A shame attack is usually experienced as a humiliating feeling that we have just shown how worthless, or stupid, or how bad we are to others. It can be a mild, moderate, or severe problem for us. If you are familiar with these experiences, please give some examples of how, when, and where these are more likely to occur for you.

_____

_____

_____

_____

_____

_____

_____

_____

Finally, describe the feelings you had while completing this section:

_____

_____

_____

_____

_____

_____

_____

_____

_____

_____

_____

_____

1.3 The Scab of Contempt

Above the *emotional "wounds"* of abandonment lies the *"infection"* of shame. Just above the infection, and closest to the surface of our awareness, is the *"scab"* of contempt.

Contempt: **a powerful feeling of dislike toward somebody or something considered to be worthless, inferior, or undeserving of respect."**

This powerful feeling can be pointed inward as self-contempt (*internalized contempt),* or it can be pointed outward as contempt for others (*externalized contempt*) such as authority figures, life in general, the world, God, etc. Most often we usually direct the contempt inward through self-talk such as, *"I'm no good, I screw everything up, I can't get anything right!"* until we have had all we can take. Then we point it outward by blowing up at someone close to us which in turn causes us to direct it back on ourselves saying, *"Boy, I've just proven it again! I hurt someone I care about."*

Some people stay primarily with internalizing their contempt, others tend to externalize contempt. *"Internalizers"* are more likely to feel and/or appear vulnerable and shameful. *"Externalizers"* are more likely to feel and/or appear demanding and act shameless and blameless. Both may feel victimized.

Internalizers turn their contempt on themselves and tend to have problems with (Check off those that apply):

- ❑ Depression
- ❑ Other-Centeredness
- ❑ Care-taking and approval-seeking
- ❑ Lack of adequate boundaries; can't say "no" (You might leave!)
- ❑ Fear of abandonment also known as a "Terror of Aloneness."
- ❑ Lack of a sense of personal power

Externalizers are less likely to be aware of their behavior and the affect it has on others. They turn their contempt outward toward others and tend to have problems with: (Check off those that apply)

- ❑ Anger and hostility
- ❑ Self-centeredness
- ❑ Being "Shameless and Blameless"— nothing is ever their fault, can't admit when they are wrong
- ❑ Intrusiveness—don't respect the boundaries of others, may use others as objects
- ❑ Rigid boundaries—You can't tell them anything, can't get through to them
- ❑ Anti-dependent—Proclaiming they don't you they don't need anyone!

Exercise - Explore the following questions in as much detail as you can. Use the back of the paper when necessary.

Are you primarily an Internalizer of contempt, an Externalizer of contempt, or a mixture of both? Explain your answer:

_____
_____
_____
_____
_____
_____
_____
_____

Describe your self-talk as it relates to the definition of contempt (above). Do you demonstrate more contempt for yourself, for others or for both? Explain:

_____
_____
_____
_____
_____
_____
_____
_____
_____

Give examples of times you have felt inappropriate guilt (i.e., guilt about things over which you have little or no control).

_____
_____
_____
_____
_____
_____

Give examples of times you have felt inappropriate anger (i.e., wanted to, or did, lash out at someone with little or no provocation).

_____
_____
_____
_____
_____
_____
_____

Finally, describe the feelings you had while completing this exercise (Appendix B feeling list):

_____
_____
_____
_____
_____
_____
_____
_____

1.4 Transactional Analysis & Ego-States

Transactional Analysis (TA) was developed by Eric Berne, MD in the 1960s. Originally, TA focused on three ego-states and studied of how people interact with each other (*Interpersonally*) from within these states. Later a second branch of TA was developed called *Structural Analysis*.

Structural Analysis studies the interaction between one's own ego-states (*Intra-personally*) and how that plays out in interactions with the ego-states of others (*Inter-personally*). It is a method of analyzing a person's thoughts, feelings, physiology and behavior based on their *ego-states*. Take, as an example of ego-states, an accountant who goes to work on time every day, is very professional, and wears a three-piece business suit. While at work he is very reserved, purposeful, and conducts the day's activities with precision—he is all business. Now witness the transformation come Friday night; he goes home, throws on his boots, blue jeans, a cowboy hat, and goes to a local "meat-market" where riding the bull and dancing the two-step run a close second only to chasing women until the wee hours of the morning. In this dramatic example, there is obviously an ego-state for work and an ego-state for play.

Most of us shift through several ego-states a day—most people refer to them as "moods." Sometimes the "mood" shifts are subtle, sometimes dramatic. Another example of an ego-state is when someone says, "One part of me wants to do X, but another part of me makes me do Y," or "I hate it when I do that!" These statements are indicative of what's known as an *internal conflict*—a *conscious part of me* wants to do one thing, but an *unconscious part of me* "makes" me do another thing.

In TA's Structural Analysis the three primary Ego-States are the *Parent Ego-State*, *The Adult Ego-State*, and the *Child Ego-State*.

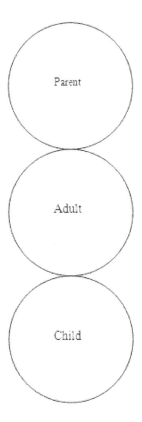

First Order Ego-State Map

The healthy Parent Ego-State is a neural network that contains the attitudes, beliefs, and behaviors "taken in" from external sources—primarily parents and authority figures. Outwardly, the Parent ES is often expressed towards others in prejudicial, critical, or nurturing behavior. Inwardly, it's experienced as old parental messages, which continue to influence the Child ES, some good messages and some limiting to the person.

The healthy Adult Ego-State is not related to a person's age. It is oriented in the present and can be comparable to a computer in that it's in charge of executive functioning, such as decision-making, problem-solving, getting the job done, etc. The healthy Adult ES is organized, unencumbered by emotions, flexible, intelligent, and functions by testing reality, estimating probabilities, and computing.

The natural Child Ego-State contains all the impulses that come naturally to a child. The Child ES is creative, adventuresome, spontaneous, curious, and affectionate. The Child ES loves to giggle, laugh, have fun and enjoy the simple things in life. It can also be a "brat" or "whine" when it doesn't get its way. The Child ES is the neural network that contains our own feelings, wants, and needs. When you see a seventy year old man sitting on a park bench enjoying an ice cream cone, he is said to be "in his Child" ego-state. When two adults are dancing "like no one is watching" they are each in their Child ego-state.

In TA theory, only one ego-state (ES) can be actively in control of the body at a given time. When a person is *"in his Child"* then that ego-state is considered "activated." In Ego-State therapy the term is "in the executive." If you have ever gotten angry, blew up, and later felt that your behavior or reaction was "childish" then you have a good idea of what is meant by "only one ego-state can have executive control at a time." In a case like this, the Adult and the Parent ego-states can be "present" in an observing role during the blow up, but only the activated child-created ego-state can have executive control of the body. When you calmed down and told yourself "that was a childish thing to do," it was coming from your Parent ES.

By the way, in TA the term "childish" is never used, the term "child-like" is used instead. "Child-like" is a respectful and more accurate way to acknowledge and own your Child ego-state. The term *Childish* is a put-down and would come from a *Critical Parent* ego-state which we will explore later.

1.4.1 Examples of Shifting Ego-States

Let's take a look at a few examples to get a clear idea of what it means to "shift ego states" during interactions with others:

Imagine a husband and wife screaming and shouting at each other like children over a disagreement. The doorbell rings and almost immediately both suddenly stop fighting. They change their expressions and tone of voice. By the time one of them answers the door; they are very calm, reasonable, and pleasant.

The couple was in their respective Child ego-states when fighting, but almost instantly put their issues aside shifting into their Adult ES when their company arrived.

Imagine a receptionist complaining bitterly to a co-worker about her job. When the phone rings, she almost instantly adopts a friendly, cheerful, can-do attitude with the person on the other end of the call, who happens to be her boss.

The Receptionist was in her Child ES when complaining, but quickly put her true feelings aside and shifted into her Adult ES with her boss on the phone.

Imagine someone trying to focus on his duties at work the day after his wife-to-be suddenly breaks off their engagement for no apparent reason. He is sad, lonely and grieving; he just wants to go home and curl up in bed.

In this example, it's difficult to make the shift from the Child ES to the Adult ES due to the emotional intensity and life changing ramifications of his fiancé leaving him. It would be even worse for someone who has abandonment issues.

1.4.2 Second Order Ego-State Map

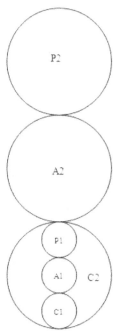

Second Order Ego-State Map

First Order Structural Analysis is looking at how two people interact with each other (interpersonally) from their various ego states. *Second Order* Analysis is useful in studying the interaction between one's own ego states (intra-personally) AND how that plays out in relationship problems (interpersonally). Everyone is born with the equipment to develop the three primary ego states. Those networks are intact, by the time we are five years old—nowhere near mature—but intact. When you see a five year old "punishing" her baby doll, she is in her Parent ES. When she is curled up in your lap, her holding her "blankie" and sucking her thumb, she is in her Child ES... When she "plays cute" to get her way ... she is in her Adult ES. Below is a "map" representing the Parent, Adult, & Child ego-states (neural networks) of a fully functioning, healthy adult. Notice that there are three ego-states within the child ego-state of the adult. This is because the adult retains the ego-states created in childhood within the Child ego-state.

The P2, A2 and C2 in Second Order Structural Analysis are the ideal healthy representations of the Parent, Adult, and Child in the fully developed and well-adjusted adult.

The healthy Parent-in-the-adult (P2) is "all-about-the-child." the P2 nurtures and protects inner states of self and others. This is strictly a healthy use of the ideal parent.

The healthy Adult-in-the-adult (A2), I call it the "CEO of the Self," because it is wise, mature, "here-and-now" focused, makes good decisions by consulting the other ego-states and generally acts on behalf of the whole person whenever executive functions must be carried out.

The healthy Child-in-the-adult (C2) is the ideal representation of a well-adjusted Child ES ... a non-wounded Child ego-state with no abandonment, shame, or contempt issues from the past.

The healthy *child-created* ego-states are listed below:
- P1 = *Parent-in-the-child* or the "Adapted Child"
- A1 = *Adult-in-the-child* or the "Little Professor"
- C1 = *Child-in-the-child* or the "Natural Child"

1.4.3 The Adapted Child (P1)

The Adapted Child ego-state is the part of the Child ego-state that contains the "training" for how to get along in the world according to the trainers—primarily Mom and/or Dad. This ego-state is the part that *adapts* to the needs or rules of society as laid down in the family, school, church, etc. There is a need for this socialization because children are born without any knowledge of how to get along in civilization. Everything about the culture, including the language must be learned. So, some of this training is necessary, helpful and even crucial.

However, sometimes we could do without the training as when wounded parents pass on their limiting beliefs, injunctions, abandonment, shame, and contempt. This leaves the child feeling very "Not-Okay." When you are being courteous, compliant, avoiding confrontation, procrastinating, or feeling Not-Okay, you're likely to be expressing your Adapted Child; the part of you that has adapted to the functioning of the family.

A child's first sense of conscience develops very slowly from interacting with their environment, especially with parents and other influential care-takers that are their teachers and role models. Smiling and other positive responses from parents convey to a child approval for doing "what's right," which is an example of positive reinforcement. Cold or angry parental responses transmit a sense of punishment or pain for doing "wrong," i.e., negative reinforcement. The Adapted Child, with the aid of their *Little Professor* (see below), discovers how to avoid pain and get approval. They *adapt* to the *"Shoulds," "Musts," and "Oughts"* of their parents and care-takers.

While all children need to learn the healthy rules of society in order to grow and thrive (self-actualization), they adapt to the dysfunction of the family through the use of survival skills (self-preservation). Children from dysfunctional families were even given specific spoken and unspoken instructions on how to adapt; in TA these are referred to as Injunctions (rules). These rules become encoded into the subconscious programming of the Adapted Child ego-state on the neural networks for survival. Here are a few examples of unhealthy injunctions:

- "Don't talk, don't think, don't feel and/or don't trust"
- "Don't be sad"
- "Don't cry, I can't stand it when you cry"
- "Don't be angry"
- "Don't be afraid"
- "Don't do better than me"

The Adapted Child ego-state, then, becomes the precise location of the emotional wounds of unmet childhood dependency needs. It is within this ego-state that the three ego-states we will refer to collectively as the *wounded inner children* exist (See below).

1.4.4 The Little Professor (A1)

The *Little Professor* is the smart little kid in each person. When you are feeling intuitive, experiencing a moment of genius, creating just for the fun of it, or manipulating someone else to get what you want, your Little Professor is likely to be involved. The Little Professor ego-state is the childhood version of the Adult ego-state which is also known in TA circles as the Professor. The main difference is that the Little Professor lacks the life experience of the Adult ego-state. The Adult ego-state has years of experience, wisdom, and maturity while the Little Professor must rely on intuition, ingenuity, instinct, and creativity.

The Little Professor intuits much of what's going on. S/he looks into the face of mom or dad and "figures out" they'd better stop what they're doing or keep doing it—depending on the expression they get. The Little Professor is either responsible for getting us into relationship problems or out of relationship problems, the former by manipulation and the latter by creativity. The Little Professor also functions to assist the Adapted Child in figuring out how to adapt.

The intuitive Little Professor is still active after a person has grown up. The Adult ego-state and the Little Professor make a good team. The Adult ego-state provides know-how, and the Little Professor provides imagination and creativity. Together they can design a new building, write a book, improve human relationships, decorate your home, and so forth.

1.4.5 The Natural Child (C1)

The *Natural Child* ego-state feels an uninhibited sense of freedom and does impulsively whatever he or she wants to do. When you're being expressive, spontaneous, affectionate, playful, selfish, or standing up for your own rights, you're very likely expressing your natural child. By nature the Natural Child is self-centered and insensitive to other people's feelings—pure un-adapted child. They can be selfish, sometimes willful, and don't like to share or take turns.

The Natural Child is the part that likes to play, explore, have adventures, giggle and laugh at simple things. Like all children, this ego-state can be fearful and have temper tantrums on occasion. It can also be the source of impulsively "leaping before they look." If parents are good teachers and role models they will help teach a child patiently and affectionately how to control their impulses by setting healthy, consistent limits. They will also be accepting of the child's needs to assert themselves and allow them to have their feelings, even when their behavior is not acceptable and must be corrected.

In the ideal situation and environment, these ego-states are flexible, working in harmony with each other and the child is said to be "well-adjusted." In moderate to severely wounded people, these ego-states are less flexible and many times in conflict with each other causing restlessness, irritability and discontent. We will explore this next.

1.5 Introducing the Wounded Inner Children

The study of Ego States through TA and Structural Analysis preceded and eventually gave birth to what has widely become known as *the Inner Child*. Dr. Charles Whitfield (1987) was the original pioneer who led the way with his Book, *Healing the Child Within*. Many other therapists, including John Bradshaw, have contributed greatly to the evolution of Inner Child therapies. In these current pages, the *"Inner Child"* or *"Inner Children"* are also metaphors for the neural networks that store the essence of various significantly intense emotional experiences—whether they are significantly happy or traumatic experiences.

As described in the first two chapters, fear of abandonment is almost always a direct result of feeling or actually being abandoned at some point in childhood. This real or perceived abandonment is traumatic to children causing fragmentations of the Self.

Let's use the analogy of a ceramic baseball to explain: Imagine an image of the core-self as if it were a ceramic baseball floating in space. Now imagine watching the ball get hit with a baseball bat. Usually an image of the baseball breaking into fragments or pieces usually comes to mind. That is a good image of what happens to the core-personality of a child who is traumatized. If the trauma is frequent or severe enough, the baseball shatters. If it is an infrequent less traumatic experience, the baseball may have a few chunks broken out of it. Now imagine the pieces and parts of the core-self floating nearby, not connected but still in the image. This image illustrates the concept of a *fragmented self*. It also illustrates how various child-created feeling-states can be frozen in time, unable to grow or be updated.

These frozen feeling-states are not connected to the core-self and, therefore, do not have access to the resources of the constantly growing/evolving core-self. They are nearby and ready to act whenever a trigger in the environment sets them off—but they can only react with the resources available to them at the time they were created. These parts-of-self or frozen feeling-states, containing the wounds of abandonment, shame, and contempt, are mapped out in the diagram below.

1.5.1 Third Order Ego-State Map

As mentioned earlier, the *Adapted Child ego-state (P1)* is the primary location of the accumulated abandonment, shame, and contempt resulting from unmet childhood dependency needs. In the diagram below, we can really begin to see ego-states, embedded in ego-states, embedded in ego-states, etc.

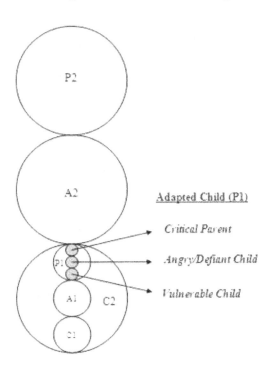

1.5.2 Abandonment and the Vulnerable Child

The **Vulnerable Child** ego-state is the part of our personality that develops first. In the ideal situation, it is the part of us that learns how to be vulnerable and emotionally available in relationships—it helps us *connect* with others. If we grew up in a dysfunctional family it is this part that also carries all the original pain of abandonment from our childhood. Infants are totally vulnerable and dependent when they are born. Very young children cannot exist as *separate* beings; they have no way to care for or defend themselves, no way to survive without being *connected* to a nurturing, protective other.

It is in this vulnerable ego-state that we first develop our ability to connect with others later in life. Issues of trust and safety are the primary developmental focus in the first two years and provide the backdrop for all the later stages of development. It is paramount that children have a "safe container" in order to develop this ability for healthy trust and sense of safety. In the ideal, the parents are to provide that safe container in the family dynamics they create and/or tolerate. Ideally, over the course of one's life one becomes more and more independent—i.e., more able to function as a *separate* being. It is in these ongoing struggles to establish a healthy balance between *separateness and connectedness* that most interpersonal and intrapersonal problems arise; including the wounding of abandonment, shame and contempt.

Prior to birth, we are almost symbiotic with our mother. We live off of her life-force, eat what she eats, feel what she feels, and are as connected as two people can possibly be connected. The rest of childhood is about separation. The first separation is the day of our birth. Now we are no longer physically joined with each other, they even cut the umbilical cord. It is a very traumatic event, but one that provides us with our first experience of being separate.

Even so, a symbiotic connection remains in the emotional attachment we have with our parents, especially mother, the first two years of life. This symbiotic attachment is analogous to an emotional umbilical cord. Imagine a transparent conduit between mother and child. This conduit exists so mother can "feed" the child the emotional supplies necessary to get a good start in life. Supplies such as love, attention, affection, adoration, and safety are conveyed to the child through holding, touch, responsiveness, availability and the primal gaze.

When the emotional umbilical cord is attached to a wounded parent, then abandonment, shame and contempt can also be transferred through this emotional connection right along with those emotional supplies. In the case of a moderate-to-severely wounded parent, more wounds may be transferred than supplies leading to difficulties in *connecting* to others later in life.

The second major separation, aka the emotional birth, comes with the "terrible two's" which is when the child begins to say "no" and/or has trouble hearing the word "no." This are a youngsters first bid for emotional autonomy (more separation). It is also our first brief glimpse of the *Angry/Defiant Child,* which we will explore shortly. How parents react to these initial and subsequent bids for autonomy is crucial to healthy development.

When healthy *separation* is not allowed, as is true with dysfunctional families, difficulty experiencing or maintaining a healthy sense-of-self can result later in life. In dysfunctional families, parents tend to be too separated (disengaged) or too connected (enmeshed) with their children. They tend to have trouble allowing and even helping their child to discover themselves and instead try to mold the child into what they want them to be. In moderate-to-severely dysfunctional family the *safe container* does not exist. Even though the dysfunction may wax-and-wane according to the level of stress, there is always a sense of impending doom because cease-fires never last. The child learns to remain hyper-vigilant, which puts them in a constant survival mode—the *fight, flight, or freeze* response always at the ready.

Remember that kids in a dysfunctional family are like POWs who cannot overtly fight or run away … so they freeze until their Little Professor can help them figure out how to flee. The only direction for them to flee is inwardly; through the use of imagination and fantasy provided by the Little Professor, they set up a safe container of their own in many creative ways.

The Vulnerable Child ego-state adapts to the dysfunction of the family by learning, mapping, and encoding creative survival skills such as people-pleasing, care-taking, getting confused, mistrust (unable to trust or trusting too much), and how to "go into hiding" in a fantasy world to name a few.

Since these are survival skills, and they are learned in a hyper-vigilant state, which adds intensity to repetition, the Vulnerable Child ego-state exists on the highly-secure self-preservation networks of the unconscious mind where they are "protected" from updates.

As a result, the survival skills of the Vulnerable Child ego-state become frozen in time—hence the term *frozen feeling-state*. When these survival strategies are triggered, one goes into a child-like state of vulnerability (flight response). The triggered person may experience fear, panic, and even terror. They may act, think, feel and behave like the child they were when they were originally wounded—even in their adult years.

1.5.3 Shame and the Critical Parent

The **Critical Parent** ego-state contains all the critical parental messages given to the child. The younger a child is the more receptive they are to these messages, referred to as injunctions and counter-injunctions in TA language. In the ideal situation parents teach their kids the things they need to know to get along in the world—including how to be a critical thinker. In a shame-based dysfunctional family, this is done through messages of *shame* and *discounting* of wants, needs, and feelings of the child. Children watch and learn from the examples given by their parents. This is called role-modeling; Dad is a model for how men are in the world and Mom is a model for how women are in the world. Together they model how men and women get along providing a model for *"how to do relationships."*

These models provided by the parents get taken-in by the child and recorded on the neural circuitry for *"how things should, must, or ought to be"* according to our parents. The ability to be a critical thinker is just as valuable as any other ego-state. However, problems arise when one grows up in a shame-based family. This Critical Parent neural network becomes the location for all the *shaming messages of the parents*; all the ways a shame-based parent *discounts* the want, needs, opinions and even the reality of the child; and all the *disapproval patterns* of the parents. Yes we need to be able to think critically, but we don't need the shaming, name-calling, belittling and abusive voice of a wounded Critical Parent looming over us all the time.

1.5.4 Contempt and the Angry/Defiant Child

Even though the "terrible two's" marks the first real appearance of the **Angry/Defiant Child** ego-state, the onset of puberty sets the stage for the official debut. One only needs to spend a little time with a twelve to thirteen year old to know what is meant by the Angry/Defiant Child ego-state. It is around that time that the ability to think abstractly and form an opinion develops—and those opinions WILL be expressed (unless it is not safe to do so).

This is the second major bid for autonomy, and it takes the child to a whole new level. The end of puberty and the onset of adolescence is just the beginning for the Angry/Defiant Child ego-state, even in the best of family circumstances. There are chemical changes in the mind and body that give a sense of power and control never before experienced. Childhood is a fairly organized period of life; parents tell the child when to get up, when to get out of bed, what to eat, what to wear, etc.—and most kids are fine with that.

Adulthood is also fairly organized; but now the young adult calls the shots on when to get up, when to go to be, what to wear, etc. On the other hand, adolescence is a period of disorganization where there is fighting, conflict, and sometimes downright chaos. There is a power struggle where the young person fights to claim more and more power, freedom, privacy, and decision making rights and the parents fight to hold onto what little control they have, usually in the best interest of the child. This period of transition is as tumultuous as it has to be in order to break the "apron strings." The harder a parent holds on, the stronger the teen will rebel. Many times leaving home is not a ceremonious occasion at all. In fact, it can be traumatic for everyone involved.

The Angry/Defiant part of us comes along to *help us separate* as demonstrated in the paragraph above. This is also an essential part of a fully functioning adult human being. The Angry/Defiant part helps us say "no," a two-letter word that sets boundaries around our physical and emotional space. These boundaries define the territory of ourselves. We teach people how to treat us by the behaviors that we tolerate and those that we don't tolerate. While saying no sets the boundaries, our follow-through is what gives it "teeth." The Angry/Defiant part of us gives us the strength and courage to protect ourselves.

It has often been pointed out that anger is never a problem—it's *how one handles anger* that can be a problem. In the ideal situation, a person has learned how to bring *just enough anger* to a situation to meet the need for that situation. If one was not allowed to have their anger as a child then they tend to portray a passive style—aka, the "doormat." If one was raised with an unrealistic sense of entitlement, they tend to adopt an aggressive style of anger—aka, the "bully." If one is raised in a safe container and allowed to have all of their feelings within healthy limits they tend to adopt what is known as an assertive style of handling anger. Passive persons give up their rights for the other, aggressive persons walk on the rights of others while standing up for their rights, an assertive person can stand up for their own rights without walking all over the right of others.

So, in the ideal situation we need the power of our Angry/Defiant part but not the contempt that comes with the wounds of abandonment. Problems with passiveness and aggressiveness are part of the package when one grows up on the battlefield of a moderate-to-severely dysfunctional family. Passive Internalizers of contempt tend to have their Angry/Defiant Child pointed inward while Aggressive Externalizers point their contempt outward at others.

On the battlefield of a dysfunctional family, with the help of the Angry/Defiant Child ego-state now the child can tap into an inner strength that helps them resist and endure the wounding process. Maybe for the first time they experience the fight response—a much more empowering state where they can feel a sense of personal safety. In this fashion, the

Angry/Defiant Child ego-state takes a protector role for the Vulnerable Child ego-state. As a *protector*, it too gets encoded on the highly-secure self-preservation networks of the unconscious mind where they are "protected" from updates. As a result, the survival skills of the Angry/Defiant Child ego-state become frozen in time—creating another *frozen feeling-state*.

When these survival strategies are triggered, one goes into a child-like state of anger and defiance. The triggered person may directly express rage and temper tantrums, or they may indirectly express anger and defiance through passive-aggressive behaviors like cancelling an important date saying, "I'm sorry, I can't go after all, I think I'm getting a headache." The person may act, think, feel and behave like the child they were when they were originally wounded. Many couples know the experience of feeling as though they and their partner behaved like children during a fight.

1.5.5 External Focus and the Little Professor

*Consisting of **the wounds of abandonment** (Vulnerable Child energy), **the infection of shame** (Critical Parent energy), and **the scab of contempt** (Angry/Defiant Child energy); the False Self is really a free-floating mass of pain and energy just beneath the surface of our awareness—just waiting to be triggered.*

Emotional pain is something children do not handle well. They do not possess the psychological equipment to understand or cope with it. They do possess some very powerful "Little Professor" defense mechanisms which help them avoid experiencing the full brunt of the pain. One of these defenses, repression, automatically stuffs the pain into the realm of the subconscious. They feel the ache but not as fully as they would otherwise. Another defense is the ability to keep an External Focus. The following is a list of distractions kids use to keep an external focus. Children also use some of these behaviors to get their needs met (as described in the roles above) and/or act out their feelings. Check the ones that apply to you:

- ☐ Fantasy/Play—Playing house for hours at a time
- ☐ Reading—comic books, love stories, etc.
- ☐ Caretaking other family members
- ☐ Talking to imaginary friends
- ☐ Video games
- ☐ Movies and Cartoons
- ☐ Hyperactive behavior
- ☐ Fighting with siblings
- ☐ Hurting family pets
- ☐ Hurting themselves
- ☐ Vandalism
- ☐ Compulsive shoplifting
- ☐ Eating too much
- ☐ Daydreaming
- ☐ Clowning and acting silly
- ☐ Taking care of a sick parent
- ☐ Taking on duties of a parent
- ☐ Placating, trying to keep others from "rocking the boat" to avoid conflict
- ☐ Others?_____

Write as much as you can about which distractions you may have used to keep an external focus in your childhood, including any that are not listed here. Furthermore, describe how effective your distractions were … i.e., did they work or was it hard to keep your focus directed outward? The effectiveness of these distractions can be measured in how much pain the child was aware of at the time.

_____
_____
_____
_____
_____
_____
_____
_____
_____

If we have a lot of repressed trauma, then we may be prone to experience "trauma echoes" which are produced by "triggers" associated with the trauma. For example, let's say a five year old boy was repeatedly molested in a dark room with the smell of garlic present ... forty years later he walks into a dark room that smells of garlic and gets flooded with all the emotions and experience of that past event. He then reacts and feels as if he is that boy at five years old again.

Other traumas may not be as striking as the above example. Sometimes the trauma-producing events are more subtle or disguised such being ignored or smothered. In these cases for example various "triggers" may produce reactions such as a need to "pursue" (for the adult who was ignored as a child) and a need to "distance" (for the adult who was smothered as a child). Pursuing is a set of behavioral reactions of the Vulnerable Child ego-state that is grounded in fear of abandonment while Distancing behaviors are an Angry and/or Defiant Child ego-state reactions grounded in a fear of being engulfed or "swallowed up" thereby losing one's sense of self.

Some traumas are even more subtle. Take, for example, when someone laughs after Bill makes a comment in the morning staff meeting. Bill suddenly finds himself in the midst of a shame attack, even though he has no indication of why the other person was laughing. In this example, Bill was unconsciously triggered to a time in his childhood when he gave his first book report in front of the class and was made fun of by other kids who were giggling and pointing at him during his presentation.

Think about times you have felt "triggered" or times when your emotional "buttons get pushed" and write about those that happen frequently or enough to recognize a pattern. Explore how these episodes may relate to your childhood experiences and, if so, how it affects you're "here and now" adult relationships, job, social life, family, etc.

_____

_____

_____

Our distractions of childhood become more sophisticated as we grow and develop. They are known as the symptoms of codependency later in life. Take a look at the list of codependent symptoms and controlling behaviors in Appendix C and identify the ones you see in yourself and in your current relationships.

_____

_____

_____

_____

_____

_____

_____

_____

_____

We do not knowingly participate in the use of repression and the development of an external focus. This is done automatically, beneath our awareness. Defenses would not be very effective if we knew we were using them. This is another example of how intricate and amazing the human mind is. You may have become painfully aware, while completing these exercises, that we are *turning your focus inward* by doing this work.

When we turn our focus inward, we begin to remember things and feel things we might not really want to remember or feel. This is the surfacing of buried or repressed trauma. This is also the reason we say it gets worse before it gets better. If this is happening to you, be aware that what you are doing is working. We must surface the pain in order to initiate the healing process of recovery. Recovery groups and individual therapies also turn our focus inward.

NOTE: *You may want to take some time to write about what you are experiencing in a journal. Also—know your limits. It is okay to take breaks or put this workbook down completely if you are not ready to do the work. Call someone if you need to talk.*

Section 2: Getting to know your "Invented Self"

In addition to the distraction technique of an external focus, another thing a child must do in order to avoid their inner world and stay in their outer world is to unconsciously build a wall between their awareness and their unawareness. These "walls" are constructed automatically of psychological defense mechanisms and ways of behaving that get a response. The walls have been collectively referred to as *"survival roles"* because their function is to help children survive in the face of unmet dependency needs.

Children learn to "cover up" their false self with these walls of defense by projecting an image other people might find acceptable. This is often referred to as "wearing a mask." I think of it as inventing a self (see "Invented Self" below) to cover up the false self because, *"If people really knew me they would not like me"* (shame), *"and they would reject me"* (fear of more abandonment).

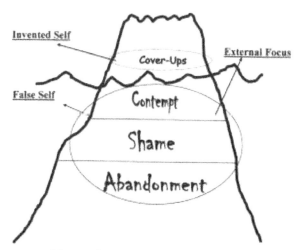

Figure: Invented Self and False Self

Children unwittingly invent and project these images, or survival roles, through the use of unconscious defense mechanisms in order to avoid the intolerable reality of their unmet needs for time, attention, affection and direction. The pain is still there, but it is not as "in their face" as it would be due to one defense known as **repression**. Repression automatically pushes the pain deep into their subconscious until the child matures enough to develop the psychological equipment to cope with it. (See "False Self" above)

Survival roles also serve to help the child find ways to get their needs for time, attention, affection, and direction met. For example, in a dysfunctional family one parent gets caught up in some form of problematic behavior while the other gets caught up with trying to control or "fix" the problem parent. They get enmeshed with each other and the problem behavior as well leaving less and less time to attend to anything else including the children.

2:1 Survival Roles, Cover-ups, and "Masks"

This wall of defenses is sometimes called a "mask," or "cover-ups." Here the wall of defenses is referred to as the "Invented Self." The invented self is not really a self at all. It is a role we learn to play in order to get some of our needs met.

For example, let's use an alcoholic family system to describe how these roles are shaped:

Parent 1: **Alcoholic**—increasingly preoccupied with the drink.

Parent 2: **Chief Enabler**—increasingly preoccupied with the drinker.

First child: **Hero**—Preoccupied with success.

Flashy Hero: Learns that getting all A's, becoming class president, being the captain of the football team or head cheerleader, are ways of getting time, attention, affection and direction. Anything less than perfect goes relatively unnoticed by the parents.

Responsible Hero: Takes over parental duties that don't get done such as cleaning house, taking care of the younger kids, doing the laundry, taking care of the alcoholic parent, etc.

Second Child: **Rebel** or **Scapegoat**—Preoccupied with trouble. The rebel cannot compete with the hero for positive attention so goes in the opposite direction and gets the negative attention by acting out. This child gets time, attention, affection from teachers, principals, counselors, juvenile officers, etc. The rebel usually gets the most attention at home because the parents are forced to deal with his/her misbehavior due to calls or visits from all the above.

Middle Child: **Lost Child**—Preoccupied with a fantasy world. Lost children cannot compete for the positive or negative attention, so they learn to get some of their needs met by creating a world of their own through play, books, toys, imaginary friends, pets, etc. In the worst cases become shy and withdrawn because they are "off in their own little world" so often they don't learn to interact with other kids much.

Youngest Child: **Mascot**—Preoccupied with humor or being cute. The baby of the family gets a lot of time, attention, affection, and direction for the cute and funny things babies do. They learn to stay "on stage" and become the class clown or the beauty queen.

While these roles look different on the outside, they cover up the same thing on the inside … that free-floating mass of pain we call the False Self.

The **Survival Roles** above do not always follow the pattern described above, but more often than not they do. The first born is usually the Hero because it is the preferred role, and they have the first crack at it. All kids want the positive attention and honor assigned to the Hero. However, if that mask is taken then they have to settle for the next best thing.

The Rebel is the second most effective role. Even though the attention is negative, they get lots more of it because the parents have to deal with this child's misbehavior so the Rebel becomes the priority.

Middle children are more likely to get Lost in the crowd, so they must sharpen their skills with fantasy in order to survive. Middle children also tend to be chameleons, switching from one survival role to another whenever the opportunity presents itself. Many times they experience all the roles in their life at one time or another.

The baby of the family is almost always the center of attention so it is not surprising that they make the most of that and become the Mascot.

So, it is *birth order, not personality, not willfulness, and not inherently bad character* that reinforces or "shapes" the original masks we learn to wear. A child does not decide to behave this way, they instinctively act-out these roles until they find the *one that works the best in getting them **the time, attention, affection and direction** they need.*

The Hero gets it from teachers, coaches, newspaper reporters, and others that are amazed by their outstanding abilities. The Rebel gets it from teachers, principals, juvenile officers, counselors, and anyone else who wants to help them get back on track. The Lost Child gets it through fantasy, and the Mascot gets it through being on stage.

These roles are also reinforced at home because they all bring something to the family, helping the system to survive as well. The Hero brings honor to the family. The Rebel brings distraction, which takes the focus off the primary dysfunction in the marital pair. This is why another term used for the Rebel is "Scapegoat." They act as a lightning rod help to keep the family intact because if the parents have too much time to face what is going on between them, they might get a divorce, and the family then disintegrates.

The Lost Child brings relief because you never have to worry about this child and hardly notice they are there. The Mascot brings entertainment and humor, diffusing the seriousness of the family dysfunction. All of these roles look different on the outside, but they are all alike on the inside—they are driven by Abandonment, Shame, and Contempt.

2.2 Impression Management

Another function of the Invented Self is to manage the impressions of others that are important to us. **Impression Management** is also known as the *"what-would-other-people-think"* syndrome. I am only "Okay" if everyone important to me thinks I'm okay.

Impression Management goes something like this:

If I have ten people in my life who are important to me and one of them is not happy with me while the other nine think I am the greatest thing in the world, I would focus much of my energy thinking about how I could get that one back in line with the others. If two or three get upset with me, I get anxious. If four or five of them don't think much of me, I get desperate or panicky because it almost feels like I am dying. It feels like I am dying because in a way I am. *I draw my identity, my sense of self, from those ten people. If I am okay with them then I feel okay.*

So, I must be vigilant in managing the impressions of those around me. If they accept me and think I'm okay I must be... right? Not necessarily, even if they accept me, I cannot truly accept their acceptance because at another level I feel like a phony. An example of this is when we have difficulty accepting compliments from others. Somewhere inside the voice of shame is telling us *"They wouldn't say that if they really knew you!"* The voice may even be inaudible, but we feel like a phony anyway. This accounts for the paradox of why we tend to discount or minimize anything positive coming from those we try to please.

2.2.1 The Five Drivers and the "Safety Net"

As outlined in the material on Script Messages (see page 116), Counter-Injunctions play a big role in development of the invented self and managing the impressions of others. The first five counter-injunctions listed below are known in TA as **"The Five Drivers"** because they "drive" us relentlessly, often underneath our awareness and against our will. Most, if not all, of the other counter-injunctions can fit into one or a combination of the first five:

- "Be Strong"
- "Be Perfect"
- "Try Hard"
- "Please Others"
- "Hurry Up"
- "Work Hard" (a combination of "Try Hard + Please Others")
- "Don't ask for what you need" (a combination of "Be Strong + Try Hard")

These five **Drivers** do just that, they "drive" survival role behaviors by providing internal pressure in the form of anxiety and stress if and when they are disobeyed or resisted. This pressure may be reminiscent of the feeling of "being in trouble" with authority figures from childhood. Conversely, these Drivers provide a "Safety Net of Okay-ness" *as long as we obey them*—As long as we *stay in the Driver behavior* we can "feel somewhat okay" because the Drivers help us ward off the shame-based messages of the Critical Parent. For example:

A **Family Hero** may be driven by an inner mandate to "Be Perfect & Be Strong" (Flashy Hero) or "Be Strong and Work Hard" (Responsible One).

A **Rebel** may be compelled to play the "tough guy or gal" in obedience to a "Be Strong" counter-injunction. A Family Scapegoat may find themselves impulsively getting into trouble over and over again, no matter how "Hard they Try" to "Please Others."

A **Lost Child** may find him or herself trapped in an abusive relationship as they carry out a compulsion to "Try Hard to Please Others and Hurry Up about it!"

And a **Family Mascot** may take responsibility for making everyone else feel good by "Being Strong and Pleasing Others by Being Perfectly cute and/or funny," thereby surrounding the family and others with a "Happy Bubble."

2.2.2 Falling Through the "Safety Net"

Now, as long as the person can keep the mask of their **Invented-Self** on by fulfilling these driver behaviors they can feel Okay. But as soon as they slip up and violate their inner mandate, even if only once, they can drop through the safety net of "Okay-ness" provided by the Driver behaviors into the territory of the **False-Self** where they experience feeling bad or "NOT Okay" anymore—also known as being "triggered" and known in TA as the "rubberband effect" because it's like being "rubberbanded" back into a childhood experience. For example:

Let's say I am a flashy **Family Hero**. When people see me coming down the hall at school they say *"Wow, that kid's got it made—he's captain of the football team, class president, an Eagle Scout AND valedictorian!"* Everybody loves me and thinks I am great. They are not aware that during my earlier years I received a "Don't Exist" injunction from one of my parents. Over time, my observant "Little Professor" notices that both parents highly value doing things right the FIRST time and working hard. So, with the creativity of my Little Professor ego-state, I figure out a way to disobey the primary injunction for suicide by making a Compound Decision something like this: *"I can exist, **so long as** I never make a mistake* (Be Perfect) *and work hard* (Try Hard and Be Strong) *all the time."*

Now I find myself with my classmates on my senior trip. It feels very awkward to me because I have spent so much time working hard and being perfect that I never learned how to "do nothing" and "just have fun." I do okay for a while because I "work hard" at succeeding socially, but finally due to a lack of experience I make a major social mistake. Others start laughing and pointing at me. Suddenly I feel very "NOT Okay" like a little kid who has been reminded he is nothing but a burden and shouldn't exist—until I can restore the Safety Net of my Driver behavior.

So, **Driver** behaviors mean: *"I can feel "Okay with me" only as long as I …"* (am *Strong,* am *Perfect, Please Others, Try hard,* and/or *Hurry Up*). When I am not able to keep up the Driver behavior, I am "triggered" into acting-out my "NOT Okay" feeling in one of the following ways *(I = I'm) (U = you're) (- = NOT Okay) (+ = Okay):*

Blaming (I+, U-): <u>Externalizing the Not Okay feelings</u> of abandonment, shame and contempt by entertaining Critical Parent (CP) self-talk about how the other(s) are "making you feel" that way. This stirs up the *Angry/Defiant Child energy* which mixes with the CP messages and is directed outward at the other(s).

In the above example, if I were to Externalize my Critical Parent messages I might get red in the face, tense my jaw and *blame* my friends, telling them that they *"...are stupid for wanting to play such childish games all the time!"* Then punish them by staying in my room for the remainder of the trip (Magical thinking: *"I'll drink this poison and watch you die!"*).

Surrendering (I-, U+): *Internalizing the NOT Okay feelings* of abandonment, shame, and contempt by giving into the inwardly directed Critical Parent self-talk about how *"... you are never going to get what you want/need, or how you are unlovable, unworthy, etc."* This, of course, is experienced as *Vulnerable/Needy Child energy.*

In the above example, if I *surrender* to the Internalized Critical Parent I might hear a message like, *"You are so stupid! How could you be so dumb?"* and feel a sick feeling in my stomach. It might even spoil my whole trip as I isolate myself to my hotel room. (Magical Thinking: *Catastrophizing; One little slip-up is a disaster!*)

Panicking (I-, U-): *Simultaneously Internalizing and Externalizing the NOT Okay feelings* of hopelessness, helplessness, and worthlessness of the futility position while experiencing Critical Parent messages about the "Not Okay-ness" of self, others, and the world at large (causing a sense of desperation and/or urgency from *rapid cycling between Vulnerable Child energy and Angry/Defiant child energy*).

Or, in the above example, I may fall into a feeling of *futility*, hopelessness and desperation, go to my room and have a panic attack while cycling through Vulnerable Child fear of abandonment and Angry Child contempt for my friends and Critical Parent humiliation and shame. (Magical Thinking: *"Can't Thinking" and Miserabilizing; "I can't stand this! I just can't go on anymore!"*)

Exercise: Write about your thoughts, feelings, and memories of how these roles may have been played and who were the actors in your family or origin. The parents do not have to be alcoholic for kids to take on these roles ... (Any family dysfunction will do):

_____
_____
_____
_____
_____
_____
_____
_____
_____

_____
_____

If you are a parent, write about your thoughts and feelings about how these roles may fit with your own children as well:

_____
_____
_____
_____
_____
_____
_____
_____
_____

Write about how you may see these roles being played by you in the "here and now."

_____
_____
_____
_____
_____
_____
_____
_____
_____
_____
_____

2.3 Your Life Script

The Inner Family of self all have roles to play in what Transactional Analysis (TA) refers to as our Life Script. These parts of self are triggered into their respective roles and each play their part in the drama we call our life. The foundation of our Life Script is laid in the earliest scenes of our life. By the time we reach adulthood we are living this script habitually in its complete form.

The most important years are what Morris Massey refers to as the Imprint Period which entails the first seven years of life. During those most formative years we encounter significant emotional events called imprint experiences or simply "Imprints." These are the experiences from which we write our script. Lifelong decisions based upon the script messages we receive from our caretakers and environment are made by the *Little Professor in the child* during this time.

2.3.1 Psychological Positions and the Okay Corral

In the world of TA children who grow up in less than nurturing homes make decisions about themselves, about life, and about other people based upon the script messages they receive. In general, these decisions become their psychological positions about self, others, and life in general.

When exploring psychological positions (also known as existential positions) it is important to keep in mind that there are first, second, and third-degree designations given to the three unhealthy positions by TA. First degree positions are intense enough to cause problems in one's life and relationships, second degree are of moderate intensity and may cause serious impairments in life functioning, and third degree, the severe extreme of a given position, may result in considerable physical and emotional harm to self and/or others such as self-mutilation, assault, homicide, suicide, etc.

The Psychological Positions fit into four categories:
1. **I'm Okay, You're Okay** (healthy position) *"life is worth living."*

This is potentially a mentally healthy position. If realistic, people with this position about themselves and others can solve their problems constructively. Their expectations are likely to be valid. They accept the significance of other people and life in general. (*Adult and Healthy Parent ego-state reaction*)

2. **I'm Okay, You're Not-Okay** (Externalizer position) *"your life is not worth much."*

This is the position of persons who feel victimized or persecuted, so victimizes and persecutes others. They blame others for their miseries. Rebellious teens and adult criminals often have this position and take on paranoid behavior which in extreme cases may lead to homicide. (*Angry/Defiant Child, and/or Critical Parent reaction*)

3. **I'm Not-Okay, You're Okay** (Internalizer position) *"my life is not worth much."*

This is a common position of persons who feel powerless when they compare themselves to others. This position leads them to withdraw, to experience depression, and, in severe cases, to become suicidal. (*Vulnerable Child and/or Critical Parent reaction*)

4. **I'm Not-Okay, You're Not-Okay** (futility position) *"life itself isn't worth much."*

This is the position of those who lose interest in living, who exhibit desperate behavior, and two in extreme cases, commit suicide or homicide. (*Vulnerable Child, Angry/Defiant Child, AND Critical Parent reaction*)

When making decisions about themselves, children may conclude:

I'm Okay / I'm not Okay
I'm smart / I'm stupid
I'm empowered / I'm inadequate
I'm good / I'm no good
I'm confident / I'm bad, unworthy
I can do what I set my mind to / I can't do anything

When making decisions about others, children may conclude:

People are Okay / People are not Okay

People are caring / People only care about themselves

Men/women are fine / Men/women are no damn good

People are generally helpful / People are out to get me

I know compassionate people / Nobody likes me

People are nice / People are mean

When making decisions about life, children may conclude:

Life is Okay / Life is not Okay

The world is safe / The world is dangerous

Life is good / Life sucks

2.3.2 Primary "Scripty" Feelings:

When we "go into Script" we cycle through familiar "NOT Okay" feelings of Abandonment, Shame, and Contempt and wonder how and why this keeps happening to us. **In TA there are five primary feelings: Mad, Sad, Shame, Scared, and Glad.**

1. *Identify and circle the "NOT Okay" feelings you frequently experience,* especially in context of the issues you are working on. Focus on those frequent feelings that leave you asking yourself, *"How did I get here again?"* or *"Why does this keep happening to me?"*

Contempt (Mad)
Angry, Annoyed, Appalled, Aggressive, Condemned, Contempt, Detest, Disgusted, Disturbed, Distant, Enraged, Furious, Hate/Hatred, Indignant, Insulted, Mad, Mean, Obnoxious, Outraged, Spiteful, Trapped, Out-of-Control

Shame
Ashamed, Conspicuous, Embarrassed, Foolish, Guilty, Unlovable, Less than, Unworthy, Worthless Shame, Persecuted Odd, Weak, Wicked, Pitiful, Remorse, Unimportant, Don't Count

Abandonment (Sad)
Abandoned, Alone, Betrayed, Cheated, Crushed, Deserted, Devastated, Depressed, Empty, Exploited, Ignored, Isolated, Sad, Left-Out, Lonely, Longing, Lost, Rejected, Hurt, Pain, Ache, Grief, Loss, Lost, Hopeless

Scared
Panicky, Afraid, Anxious, Hysterical, Fear/Fearful, Frightened, Petrified, Restless, Jumpy, Tense, Uneasy, Worried, Fretful, Scared, Hyper-vigilant

Glad

Cheerful, Ecstatic, Excited, Glad, Happy, Hopeful, Inspired, Joy/Joyful, Love/Loved, Peaceful, Blessed, Fortunate, Overjoyed, Pleasant, Pleased, Warm, Wonderful, Terrific, Satisfied

Numb

Disconnected, Numbed-out, Confused, Foggy, Spacey, Zoned-out, Distracted, Separate, Disengaged, Cutoff, Different, Unreal, Alienated, Dissociated, Absent-minded

2. Choose a small cluster of feelings that go together, and describe in detail *one or two recent memories and one or two past memories* **that are typical** of times when you experienced these problematic feeling(s). *"Who, What, Where, When, and How's."*

_____

_____

_____

_____

_____

_____

_____

_____

_____

_____

_____

3. Where do you experience the feeling(s) in your body? Describe the physical sensations (*e.g., butterflies in my stomach, heaviness in my chest, clenched jaws, etc.*).

_____

_____

_____

_____

_____
_____
_____

4. Self-Talk and Beliefs: What thoughts and inner dialogue do you experience as you feel those feelings?

_____
_____
_____
_____
_____
_____

What "Mind Movies" or Fantasy Scenarios do you watch running through your mind during these times? What is the worst-case scenario? Best-case scenario?

_____
_____
_____
_____
_____
_____

Behavioral Reactions: What do you do, *how do you react*, to all of the above?

_____
_____
_____
_____
_____
_____
_____
_____

2.3.3 The Okay Corral

We all shift through each of these positions in various situations. If we grew up in a less-than-nurturing family we will notice that the Vulnerable Child part of our personality holds and *"I'm NOT Okay; You're Okay"* position, the Angry/Defiant part usually holds an *"I'm Okay, You're NOT Okay"* position, and the Critical Parent part can hold both positions.

Transactional Analyst Franklyn Ernst designed a way to track shifts from one position to another called the Okay Corral. This is also a way to track our shifts in ego-states as well. In the diagram below, consider the layout to be similar to a window with four panes.

The outside frame of the window represents the four positions:

The upper left is the combination of the *"I'm NOT Okay with me, you are Okay with me"* positions Ernst also calls the "Get Away From" (GAF) position where I am NOT feeling Okay and must "get away from" the "Okay" person(s) or situation (e.g., a public speaking engagement or job interview or conflict with my partner).

The upper right is the combination of the *"I'm Okay with me, you are Okay with me positions"* is the "Getting on with" (GOW) position where everyone is Okay and "getting along with each other.

The lower right pane is the combination of the *"I'm Okay with me, you are not Okay with me"* positions, where I feel Okay and must get rid of the person(s) I deem NOT Okay.

The lower left is the combination of the *"I'm NOT Okay with me, you are NOT Okay with me"* positions—the Futility position where we are "getting nowhere with" each other.

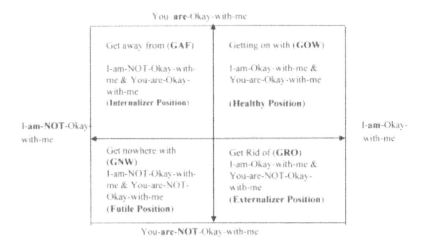

2.3.4 "Scripty" vs. Adult Operations

In TA the Term **"Scripty"** refers to a state of being "in script." This is also known as a state of being "triggered" into an inner child reaction. The alternative to being "in script" is to be "autonomous" whereby you can bring the full power of your Adult ego-state and all its problem-solving, information-gathering, and decision-making resources to bear on the here-and-now situation in which you find yourself. In other words, the inner children are NOT "driving your bus" when you are autonomous.

The following are scenarios where you can see examples of a "Scripty" operation vs. and Adult operation. (An "operation" is "how we operate" in a given situation.)

Get away from (GAF) Scenario: I am very busy at work and I notice Bill heading right for me. I've seen that look before and I know that he is bringing his current upset with him to tell me all about it and ask for advice. I don't have the time or the inclination to go through it as I am working against a deadline.

Scripty Operation: I experience a familiar Vulnerable Child feeling and adopt the *"I-am-not-Okay, you're-Okay"* position, get a sick feeling in my stomach, and say to myself, *"I just can't cope with this today; I'm not up to it!"* *"Why does this always happen to me?"* *"I have to get out of here!"* I mumble something about the bathroom, get up and leave. It is not until I am out in the hall that I can relax and collect myself. I have just reinforced my Psychological Position that *"I am not Okay, and others are Okay."*

Adult Operation: If I notice the trigger and choose to stay in my Adult ES, I might say to myself *"I am not willing to listen to Bill right now."* *"He's got problems, but it's not my job to settle them; my job is to get this report done on time."* As Bill sits down and begins to talk, I gather my papers and say, *"Hey, Bill, that sounds bad; can't talk right now though. I have to get down the hall and check some sources for this report I am working on. I hope you get this sorted out."* Then I walk out. I have chosen the healthy *"I'm-Okay, You're-Okay; Getting Away From"* operation from my Adult Ego-State.

Get Rid Of (GRO) Scenario: A little while later I am back at my desk and my secretary comes in to tell me she forgot to drop off an important package with the Fed-Ex guy and it has to arrive ASAP. She apologizes and asks what I want her to do about it.

Scripty Operation: I experience a familiar Angry Child or Critical Parent feeling and adopt the *"I-am-Okay, you're-not-Okay"* position, tense my jaw and put a furrow in my brow as I snap back, *"REALLY?! —What do you do about it?"* *"You figure this out right away and get it taken care of!"* *"And I don't want to hear from you until it's done ... understand??* I have just "Gotten rid of" my secretary as I say to myself, *"Here we go again; people just can't be trusted when it really matters!"* I then experience the emotional charge that comes with the confirmation of my Psychological Position that *"I am Okay, and others are not Okay."*

Adult Operation: If I notice the trigger and choose to stay in my Adult ES, I might say to my secretary *"Well, it's your job to figure that out; I am working on an urgent report right now." "Go find a way to take care of this and come back to let me know when it's done."* I look back down at my report signaling that our talk is over. I have "gotten rid of" my secretary from the healthy position of *"I'm Okay, and you're Okay"* even though the situation is not acceptable. In either operation, if I stop what I'm doing and "figure it out" *for her* it implies she is "NOT Okay" to take care of it herself, discounting her Adult ego-state problem solving skills.

Getting Nowhere With (GNW) Scenario: Just as my deadline is approaching and I am finishing up my report the phone rings. It's my wife. The washing machine sprung a leak. It leaked all over the floor before she could bail all the water out in the sink.

Scripty Operation: I experience a combination of Vulnerable Child & Angry Child or Critical Parent feelings and adopt the *"I-am-not- Okay, you're-not-Okay, nothing is okay"* position of futility. I tense my jaw, put a furrow in my brow, and get a sick feeling in my stomach as I say to *myself "I just can't take this after the day I've had! I can't even rely on my partner!"* I then just hang up on my wife while experiencing the helplessness and hopelessness that comes with the position of *"I'm NOT Okay, others are NOT Okay, and Life is Not Okay!"*

Adult Operation: If I notice the trigger and choose to stay in my Adult ES, I might say something like *"Okay, the damage is already done; let's just wait until I get home in an hour or so and we'll figure it out together."* I have chosen to "get nowhere with" my wife for the time being from the healthy position of *"I'm Okay, and you're Okay"* even though this situation is not acceptable.

Exercise: Using the diagram below, spend the next few days and weeks tracking your shifts between Scripty and Adult Operations by placing a dot or an X in the appropriate window pane whenever you notice you have just "gone into script" or had a triggering episode.

Notice how often you can catch yourself and switch to an Adult operation appropriate to the situation and use another symbol to track those accomplishments! Practice, practice, practice—you will get better and better. Do this exercise until you can catch yourself automatically and "shift on the fly" into your Adult ego-state.

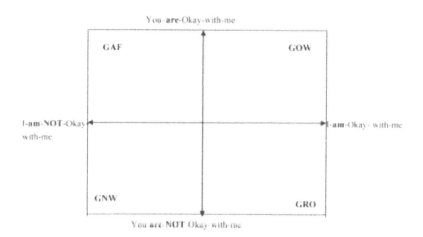

2.3.5 Script Messages: Injunctions

Injunctions are script messages sent directly or indirectly from the **Child-in-the-parent** to the **Child-in-the-child** that instruct the child what not to do. In their book, *Changing Lives through Redecision Therapy,* Robert Goulding, MD and Mary McClure Goulding, MSW, have listed **12 Basic Injunctions** to look for when working on change. They are listed below (Circle those that you can relate to, even if you can't put it into words):

- **"Don't ..."** *Example:* Fearful, over-protective parents say don't climb trees, don't run, don't try, don't go too far, don't pay rough, don't go too high on the swings, etc. These parents also tend to do everything for the child. The child gets the message that they must be fragile, or incompetent, and/or every decision they face is critical and, therefore, has trouble making decisions.

- **"Don't Exist"** Some verbal examples of how children receive this message are:
    - "If it weren't for you children, I could divorce your father..."
    - "You were a mistake"
    - "See what you do, why do you put me through this!"
    - "I wish you'd never been born!"

  The message can also be delivered in a multitude of non-verbal ways, such as how the parent cares for and holds the child, the facial expressions and tone of voice, frowns, scowls, etc.

- **"Don't Be Close"** *Example:* Discouraging the child from coming close, a lack of attention and affection, lack of physical touching, and a lack of positive strokes all send signals that may be interpreted as "Don't Be close." Also, losing several people who have been close may be enough for a child to decide it is not worth getting close because "People I care about always leave me." Or a parent was aloof and distant, modeling "Don't be Close."

- **"Don't Be Important"** *Examples:* This injunction comes from messages like "kids are to be seen, not heard," "Keep your mouth shut at the dinner table," or other discounts about how they may nothing of importance to offer. Children who are made fun of because of how they look, their race, or their social status may experience this injunction … unless they have made other decisions to "show everyone" how good they are.

- **"Don't Be a Child"** *Example:* Children who have been assigned the role of taking care of the younger children may have lost or given up their own childhood. They continue to function without the childlike qualities they have not yet developed. Other methods of conveying this message include telling a five year-old to "grow up!" or giving a toddler positive strokes for being "little men" or "proper little ladies"

- **"Don't Grow"** *Example:* The baby of the family often is the recipient of this Injunction, especially when the empty nest is approaching. This is usually the case when there is not a lot of intimacy between the parents or in single parent situations. Fathers may send this message to their daughters when they refuse to allow make-up, dating, wearing certain clothes when it is really an age-appropriate thing to do.

- **"Don't Succeed"** *Example:* A father may send the message to "not do better than me" by quitting when his son begins to win at the game they are playing. Expecting perfection or frequently saying things like "You can't do anything right!" or "What the hell is wrong with you?" are other ways this message gets conveyed.

- **"Don't Be You"** *Example:* Children who get the message they are not the sex that was preferred by their parents adopt this Injunction. A mother with four boys who wanted a girl may subconsciously make the youngest one her "daughter." Or a father with all girls may make one of them a "little buddy" by giving positive strokes for doing son-like activities.

- **"Don't Be Sane"** *Example:* Children who grow up with a parent or parents who have a mental illness can learn how to do mental illness through role modeling. They may also be negatively stroked for healthy thinking and positively stroked for silly or bizarre behaviors. Most often, double-bind messages from parent to child where the child is "damned if s/he does and damned if s/he doesn't" can foster this injunction.

- **"Don't Be Well"** *Example:* Some children only experienced nurturing when they were sick. They grow up to use the sick role to gain attention of others and to self-nurture as well. Usually at a subconscious level, getting well would mean isolation and abandonment to someone with this Injunction.

- **"Don't Belong"** *Example:* Children who move a lot are most often the ones who have learned not to attach to a social group because as soon as they make attachments they move again and have to start all over. Other circumstances include kids who were frequently put down or made fun of for one reason or another by other kids. Or maybe the parent demonstrated how to be an outsider through role modeling.

When a child accepts these script messages, their "Little Professor" DECIDES to implement a survival rule that fits the form of *"I mustn't..."* Such as *"I mustn't belong," "I mustn't be well," "I must never do better than Dad,"* etc. These decisions become **Primary Injunctions** embedded as subconscious programming. If the child "spits out" the message, then no harm is done. Intensity and repetition can have a lot to do with accepting or rejecting injunctions.

When **Injunctions** and other accepted script messages are disobeyed the person experiences the same fear, stress, and/or anxiety they felt when they were "in trouble" as a child. Injunctions are usually accepted prior to being able to use language. Pre-verbal primary injunctions are "felt" as a pressure to obey "without words."

Most of the above **12 Injunctions** are delivered and accepted in the pre-verbal years. This is a good way to tell the difference between Injunctions and Counter Injunctions (see below). Some examples of unspoken, post-verbal script messages resulting in primary injunctions include the four unspoken rules of a dysfunctional family as outlined by Claudia Black and others: (Circle those you can relate to, even if you can't put it into words):

- **"Don't Talk"** – Some reasons kids learn not to talk about problems include:
  - "If I don't talk about it then it won't hurt and will go away"
  - Parents give negative strokes for bringing it up

- o Abandonment of needs creates fear of abandonment for displeasing the parent
- o There is shame about what is going on
- o The child is directly told not to talk about it
- o Other family members role-model not talking by "ignoring" reality
- o No one knows how to talk about it

- **"Don't Trust"** – Kids may learn not to trust due to one or more of the following:
  - o Broken Promises
  - o Unpredictability
  - o Emotional Unavailability of the parents who are preoccupied with the problem or each other.

- **"Don't Feel"** – or "Don't feel that…" or Don't feel what you feel, feel what I feel." Kids may learn not to feel due to one or more of the following:
  - o Expressions of fear, sadness, anger, guilt, embarrassment, loneliness are not allowed because they may trigger the same in the parent
  - o The Little Professor in a child builds walls to protect against these feelings
  - o Learning to emotionally "Numb Out" creates physical, emotional and psychological safety

- **"Don't Think"** – or "Don't Think that…" or Don't think what you think, think what I think." Kids may learn not to feel due to one or more of the following:
  - o Mutual Denial—everyone ignores "the elephant in the living room"
  - o Parents discount the child's reality—"*Your father's not drunk! He has the flu...Don't you ever say that again!*"

- o "You don't know what you're talking about!"
- o Through fantasy the child develops their own system of denial to create a false sense of security.

Exercise: Keeping in mind that Injunctions are usually experienced as an inner pressure to obey, rather than words you "hear" in your self-talk, go over each of the Injunctions you circled above and look for evidence and examples of how they may be active in your current life and relationships. Don't be afraid to rephrase or reword them to suit your experience.

_____

_____

_____

_____

_____

_____

_____

_____

_____

_____

_____

_____

_____

_____

_____

_____

_____

_____

2.3.6 Script Messages: Counter-Injunctions

Counter-Injunctions are the result of script messages from the Parent-in-the-parent telling the Parent-in-the-child what to do and what not to do. These beliefs form the foundations for the _"Should," "Must," and "Ought to"_ rules that we develop about "how things are" in the world. **Some Counter-Injunctions** are good and helpful (Don't play in the street!)

while others become limiting beliefs that can sabotage our relationships and life goals (Men are Pigs! or "Women can't be trusted!).

Originally it was thought that *Counter-Injunctions* always ran *counter* to primary injunctions. However, it was later discovered that sometimes these script messages from Parent-to-Parent ego-states sometimes reinforce Injunctions and sometimes are irrelevant to Injunctions altogether.

We get thousands and thousands of these "shoulds" "musts" and "ought to's" during the course of our childhood. Remember the main difference between injunctions and counter-injunctions is that the latter come with words and self talk. The former are felt as pressure to comply, usually without words. Below is a partial list of examples of counter-injunctions:

- Don't air the family's dirty laundry
- Big boys don't cry
- Don't show you care
- Look both ways before you cross the street
- If it sounds too good to be true … it probably is
- Don't ask for what you need
- Be Strong
- Work Hard
- Be Honest
- Keep your word

The Five Drivers:

The first five counter-injunctions listed below are known in TA as "The five Drivers" because they "drive" us relentlessly and most if not all other counter-injunctions can fit into one or a combination of the first five:

- "Be Strong"
- "Be perfect"
- "Try Hard"
- "Please me"

- "Hurry Up"
- "Work Hard" (a combination of "Try Hard + Please Me")
- "Don't ask for what you need" (a combination of "Be Strong + Try Hard")

Exercise: Go back and review the work you did on pages 103-104. Identify which of the above "Drivers" has the most power in your life and relationships; then choose a second and a third if possible, prioritizing which ones motivate and "drive you." Remember that obeying the Driver keeps the Critical Parent quiet, but violating the Driver stirs up the Critical Parent energy causing us to *"fall through the safety-net"* into the "NOT Okay" feelings of abandonment, shame, and contempt in the False Self:

_____

_____

_____

_____

_____

_____

_____

_____

_____

_____

_____

_____

_____

Remember some times when you were "triggered" and "fell through the safety net" of your primary Driver behaviors. Which of the positions did you "land in"—was it the Blaming position? Surrendering position? Panic position? Or was there a combination of positions? (See page 100) What bad feelings did you experience? (See page 103)

_____

_____

_____

_____

_____

_____

_____

_____

Now, notice if you can identify a pattern when you get triggered—e.g., one may initially fall into the *Blaming* position and lash-out; then a bit later, shift position by *Surrendering* to the shame-based Critical Parent messages for lashing out and losing control. Describe your patterns and the resulting "Scripty" feelings below:

_____

_____

_____

_____

_____

_____

_____

_____

_____

_____

_____

_____

_____

_____

_____

_____

2.3.7 Compound Decisions

Coupling primary Injunctions with *Counter-Injunctions* create Compound Decisions:

- "Don't" ... *"Be Careful"*
- "Don't Think" ... *"Drink"* (Be strong)
- "Don't Think" ... *"Be Confused"* (Please me)
- "Don't Be a Child" ... *"Work Hard"* (Try Hard + Be Perfect)
- "Don't Be Close" ... *"Be Strong"*

- "Don't Ask for Strokes" (Don't be Close) ... *"Be Needless"* (Be Strong)
- "Don't Give Strokes" ... *"Be Withholding & Aloof"* (Be Strong)
- "Don't Relax" ... *"Hurry Up"*

Compound Decisions (also known as survival strategies) are devised by the creativity of the Little Professor into a form such as "In order to _____ I mustn't _____, I must instead_____" and then programmed into the brain. For Example:

"In order to be part of a group (belong), I mustn't be close, I must hide my feelings" (Be Strong)

"In order to exist, I mustn't relax, I must work hard all the time"

In real time, these statements are usually subconscious so that the person only experiences the pressure to obey. When these decisions are disobeyed, they can produce the same anxiety as experienced when "in trouble" during childhood. The discomfort caused by non-compliance reinforces the injunctions over time, thereby making them even stronger.

Over time, the original decisions are deeply embedded in the subconscious so that we find ourselves experiencing only the self-talk (*Italics Below*) and wondering "why am I like this?"

- **"Don't..."** – *"I can't decide." "I need someone to decide for me."*
- **"Don't Succeed"** – *"I can't do anything right." "I'm stupid." "I'll never win anything."*
- **"Don't Be Well or Sane"** – *"I must be crazy." "My condition is beyond hope, I can never get better."*
- **"Don't Feel"** – *"Emotions are a waste of time, what's the point?"*
- **"Don't Feel That"** – *"I'll never feel angry...anger is dangerous or disgusting."*

- **"Don't Feel What You Feel...Feel What I Feel"** –
  "I don't know what I feel." "How should I feel?"
  "How would you feel, if you were me?"

Exercise: Identify your Compound Decisions: Choose an Injunction from above and fill in the remaining blanks after placing the injunction in item #1 below:

1. Identify a Script Message (Injunction)

_____

(Don't...)

2. Determine the Script Decision

_____

(I mustn't...)

3. Identify observations that the Little Professor may have used back then to override the Script Decision.
"Dad/Mom/Others seem to highly value or want me to

_____ "
(Observation)

"Therefore, I or it (prohibited behavior) may be acceptable so long as _____ "
(Counter Injunction)

4. Identify the Compound Decision by combining the Injunction with the Counter Injunction:
"I can _____ *so long as I* _____ "
    (Response to Item #1)   (Counter Injunction – above)

5. Identify the feelings and sensations you experience when you don't perform the counter-Injunction:

"When/if I don't _____ *I feel* _____ "
    (Counter Injunction)   (Scripty Feelings)

2.3.8 Script Messages: Programs

Programs are script messages sent from the Adult-in-the-Adult of the parent to the Adult-in-the-Child of the child (*Little Professor*). Programs are all of the *"How to..."* instructions we get about life from our parents. The fit into the form of *"Here's how to..."* For example:

- "Here's how to cook a meal"
- "Here's how to ride a bike"
- "Here's how to fix an engine"
- "Here's how to hide your feelings"
- "Here's how to do relationships"
- "Here's how to behave in public"
- "Here's how to mess up your life"
- "Here's how to not think"

Parents send these script messages directly with words and indirectly with role-modeling. A counter-injunction frequently heard in families is "do as I say, not as I do." But, of course that's not possible for the child even though it's good advice sometimes.

Often times parents do their best to teach their kids with words and instructions, only to sabotage their own efforts by not demonstrating what they are teaching. The only way to demonstrate what they are teaching on a regular basis is to do the work outlined here.

Contaminations of the Adult Ego-State:

Technically, the Adult Ego-State is healthy and "here and now" focused with access to all of our adult resources, wisdom, and problem-solving abilities. So, when one of our *"Here's How ..."* messages is limiting and obviously originated from the wounded shame-based messages of our parent, then that message was really from the Little Professor rather than the Adult ego-state. One way to tell if the *"Here's how to..."*

message is a contamination is to look for prejudice, magical thinking, shame-based, or other thinking errors that do not stand up to the objective logic of a healthy Adult ego-state.

When that happens the concept of contamination is to blame—the Adult ego-state of the parent is considered to be "contaminated" by one of their child ego-states (the Little Professor) and they passed on a survival strategy rather than a useful adult program. It is not useful as an adult program because the primary problem-solving tool of the Little Professor is magical thinking rather than the cause-and-effect thinking of a healthy adult.

Key Point: Compound Decisions were made by the Adult-in-the-Child ego state (the Little Professor) in order to adapt to the dysfunction of that time in their life. They were made with the very limited resources available to the child at the time. Then they become embedded in the implicit memory as a subconscious program—automatic responses that can cause problems for an adult later in life. *In order to break free of these old programs that are no longer needed, the Child ego state needs to revisit and re-decide this issue. Many times therapy is needed for this.*

2.3.9 The Permission Message:

As described above Injunctions are **COMMANDS** about what to do and what not to do. In order to overcome these old script messages, we need to "re-decide" them from our Child Ego-State. When we find ourselves triggered into old behavior and decisions we need to recognize it and give ourselves permission to change.

Permission is an **INVITATION** to do things differently rather than a **COMMAND**. Our parents surely gave many Permissions about what is okay to do … *"It's okay to stand up for yourself"; "It's okay to be upset as long as you are respectful."* In fact, there are so many Permissions given by parents that it would take too much time to go over them all.

In therapy and recovery activities, Permission is a message must be given from our Adult and Parent ego-states to our

Child Ego-States. The Permission message is in the form of *"It's okay to ..."*

The Permission message needs to be delivered to the triggered Child ego-state so that the affected ego-state has the opportunity to re-decide and disobey the old COMMAND. If we don't focus with precision like this, it can be like putting a Band-Aid on the hand when it's the knee that's been scraped. Simple affirmations from the Adult Ego-State are helpful but the affected part of our personality needs to actually experience breaking free of the Injunctions and mastering the emotional bind.

Usually it is the Vulnerable Child that needs to choose to "re-decide" old issues and to adopt the new ways. This requires Permission from the Adult ego-state and help from the Angry/Defiant child ego-state. The Vulnerable Child needs to borrow enough energy from the Angry Child to Stand up for him or herself. This is usually done in imagery work where the person can be triggered and bridge back to a memory, step into the memory, be that child again and ***deliver the Redecision*** to their parent in first person:

"Don't Succeed" – *"Mom, I can and I will succeed at many things! Even if that means I will be doing better than you." "I have already succeeded in many ways." "I can also fail sometimes and not fall apart because failure is only feedback"*

"Don't Feel" – *"Dad, I am going to allow myself to have my feelings ... all of them! Even if it means you will think less of me for it – because that's about you and your misunderstandings about life – and I don't have to own it."*

"Don't Be Close" – *"Mom and Dad, I understand you've both been hurt very much and that you have only tried to protect me. But, from now on, I am going to allow others to get close to me and take my own risks. Even if that means some rejection and pain before I actually find what I'm looking for."*

Exercise: Look back over your work and choose at least one Permission Message from your Adult self to your Child ego-state in the form of "It's Okay to ..."

_____

_____

_____

_____

_____

_____

_____

_____

Choose at least one first person Redecision Message to be delivered from your Child Ego-state to the relevant parent based upon your Permission Message(s) above:

_____

_____

_____

_____

_____

_____

_____

_____

2.4 Script Element Coping Styles

2.4.1 Give In to Script Elements *(Repetition Compulsion)*

- Reliving past relationships perhaps as an unconscious attempt to "fix" them. In reality, it only strengthens the script and confirms one's beliefs about self, others, and life (Psychological Positions)
- Usually "Internalizers" use this compliant, surrendering coping style
- Frequently the *Angry/Defiant Child* ego-state is partially disowned or discounted while the *Vulnerable/Needy Child* ego-state is experienced
- Surrenderers unknowingly choose partners who tend to treat them like the parent or parents who sent the original script messages and injunctions
- They then tend to relate to partners in a compliant, passive way which reinforces the script; they relate from the wounded child ego-state while their partner relates from the critical parent ego-state.

2.4.2 Avoidance: *(aka, Denial)*

- Seeking comfort and relief for self-soothing is an ego-state strategy created by the *Little Professor* meant to help the person attempt to live without awareness of their thoughts and feelings so as not to trigger the script element.
- With this coping style thoughts and feelings are cutoff or blocked so that the person can avoid thinking about or fully experiencing the pain.
- Psychological numbing: When thoughts and feelings begin to surface they rarely go beyond an uneasiness or a sense of anxiety before they are automatically pushed back down (suppressed)
- *Both Internalizers and Externalizers* may use this avoidant coping style and tend to use objects and

activities as distractions and relief from inner pressure of "unknown" origins. (*Addictions, Obsessions, and Compulsions*)

- This coping style is frequently at the root of resistance in therapy; the Little Professor uses various techniques to block access to thoughts and feelings such as confusion, spacing out, zoning out, getting a headache, etc.

2.4.3 Fight Against the Script Elements: *(aka, Reaction Formation)*

- This coping style helps fight the pain of the script by outwardly acting, thinking, and feeling as though the opposite were true; i.e., people who have an under-achiever script element may be perfectionists; those who feel inferior may come off as grandiose or superior, etc. (they may or may not be aware of an opposite inner state)
- "Externalizers" use this coping style and frequently disown most of their *Vulnerable Needy Child* energy while embracing their *Angry or Defiant Child*.
- This coping style helps one avoid conscious awareness of pain by feeling the opposite; yet the pain exists waiting there at the subconscious level.
- Over-compensators also tend to use objects and activities as distractions and relief from inner pressure of "unknown" origins.

Exercise: Think about times in your life when you've been triggered into a scripty behavior or episode of abandonment, shame, and contempt ... Do you tend to lash out from the Angry Child, or do you defiantly "dig your heels in," or do you turn your criticism inward on your Vulnerable Child ego-state? Do you shift between one and the other in a pattern you identified in other exercises?

_____
_____
_____
_____
_____
_____
_____
_____

If you had to choose one of the three Coping Styles above as you "default" setting, which would it be and what do you know about why that is? Which Coping Styles fit each of your parents?

_____
_____
_____
_____
_____
_____
_____
_____
_____
_____
_____
_____
_____

Which of your Driver behaviors affect your choice of the above Coping Styles? Which Drivers would you guess caused your parents to choose their Coping Style?

_____
_____
_____
_____
_____
_____

_____

_____

_____

_____

_____

_____

2.5 Mini-Script Processes

According to TA theorists such as founder Eric Berne, Taibi Kahler and other TA authors (Stewart and Joines, 1987), there are only six main patterns of **Script Process.** They are listed below. These script processes seem to be universal from one culture to the next. No matter what race of nationality, these six themes are being played out over and over.

Each of us do all of these script processes from time to time. But it appears that we each have our favorites. While over the course of our life we play out our script over time … we also play out mini "versions" of the overall theme, sometimes from minute-to-minute; hence, the term "Mini-Script" Process.

2.5.1 Until Motto: "I can't have fun _until_ I've finished my work"

Principle: Something good can't happen until something less good has been finished. (And there's always something that needs to be done.)

Examples:

- Once the kids grow up and leave I'll be able to take time for me
- Life begins after forty
- After I make a fortune, then I can retire, travel and enjoy life
- After I fully understand myself then I can change

2.5.1 After Motto: "I'll have fun today but *I'll pay for it tomorrow*"

Principle: The sentence begins with a "high," then there is a fulcrum (usually the word 'but') followed by a "low." *Examples:*

- Have your fun now, after you get married the honeymoon is over"
- Wow, this is a great party! But I am going to be sick as a dog tomorrow!"

2.5.3 Almost Motto: "I almost made it this time!"

Principle: Great at starting something, gets almost done, but doesn't finish. *Examples:*

- Type One: Like pushing a big rock up a hillside, gets almost to the top, loses grip and it rolls back down again
- Type Two: Like pushing a big rock up a hillside, notices a bigger rock and taller hillside and jumps to that one, letting the other roll back down again

2.5.4 Always Motto: "Bad things always happen to me"

Principle: "If something can go wrong it will."
Examples:

- "Why do I always miss out on the fun?"
- Why does this always have to happen to me?"

2.5.5 Never Motto: "I will never get what I want or need"

Principle: "The more I want it, the more I can't have it."
Examples:

- I'll never get that promotion
- I'll never find anyone to love me

2.5.6 Open-Ended: *Variation on the "Until" and "After" themes* in that there is a Tipping Point after which things change. But after that cutoff there is a big empty void—

Example:

- "After" finishing a project the person flounders, not knowing what to do next ... "Until" another project comes along.

2.5.7 Script Drivers & Mini-Script Processes

Script Drivers also seem to be paired with the six script processes. When you discover one it is highly likely that you have the counter-part as well. The Script Allowers are Permission Messages you can give yourself from your Adult and Parent Ego-state. This requires that you learn to turn off or ignore the Critical Parent voice. The typical combinations are listed below.

Drivers Scripts	"Allower" Examples:
Be Perfect!	(Until)You're already good enough!
Please Others! yourself!	(After) It's okay to please
Be Strong!	(Never)Be open, express your wants!
Try Hard!	(Always) Do it and get what you want!
Please Others! + Try Hard!	(Almost Type 1) It's okay to take a break!
Be Perfect! + Try Hard!	(Almost Type 2) That's good enough!
Be Perfect! + Please Others!	(Open-ended) Take time to celebrate and rest!
Hurry-Up!	Relax and Take your time!

How many of these mini-script processes and Drivers can you relate to in your current life? Which one or ones are most familiar to you? Where do you suppose the Driver and Process came from? Which mini-scripts and Driver combinations can you identify in your parents? Which "Allowers" do you need to memorize and use from you Adult ES?

_____

_____

_____

_____

_____

_____

_____

_____

_____

_____

_____

_____

_____

_____

_____

_____

2.6 Abandonment-Based Script Elements

2.6.1 Self-Care Scripting:

The original pain of unmet childhood dependency needs for time, attention, affection, and/or direction can lead to issues around self-care. We tend to care for ourselves in our adult lives as we were cared for in our childhood. **Self-Care** means ensuring that I get enough sleep, eat right, exercise, and get proper healthcare. It also involves activities of daily living such as proper hygiene, living in clean and organized surroundings, and wearing clean and acceptable clothing.

If I did not get the proper time, attention, and direction in these areas growing up one element of my overall Life Script might include inadequate self-care if my Little Professor sets up a repetition-compulsion whereby I give-in to the programming I received and repeat the same neglectful behaviors—abandoning my needs as I was taught. Conversely, if I tend to fight against my programming my Little Professor will use the defense mechanism of reaction-formation and I will tend to obsess over self-care in some fashion. I may develop worries, anxieties, and fears (WAFs) around dirt and germs, how I look, am I getting sick, etc. I may also obsess over "What if" scenarios such as losing all my money and becoming homeless.

Exercise: If you suspect this is an issue for you, on the continuum below place an X on the line where you estimate that you "default" setting is for Self-Care. You may tend to slide up and down depending on the context or situation, put the X where you tend to be most often or on average.

Inadequate Self-Care		Obsessive Self-Care

If this is or was an issue for you, explore how so and identify which of the Drivers and Mini-Scripts may be active in driving

your behavior. Do you tend to fight the script you were given, avoid it altogether, or do you tend to give-in to it? Which "Allowers" do you need to employ here? Finally, if it was an issue for either of them, answer these same questions as it relates to each of your parents.

_____
_____
_____
_____
_____
_____
_____
_____
_____
_____

2.6.2 Ego-Strength Scripting:

Ego-Strength is defined as "...the ability to maintain the ego by a cluster of traits that together contributes to good mental health. The traits usually considered important include tolerance of the pain of loss, disappointment, shame, or guilt; forgiveness of those who have caused an injury, with feelings of compassion rather than anger and retaliation; acceptance of substitutes and ability to defer gratification; persistence and perseverance in the pursuit of goals; openness, flexibility, and creativity in learning to adapt; and vitality and power in the activities of life."

Our own Ego-Strength is heavily influenced by the parenting we received. Frequently in dysfunctional families one parent is a dominant, demanding and rigid **Externalizer** while the other is submissive, surrendering, **Internalizer** with low ego-strength. This set up leaves our Little Professor with a choice—which do I want to be? A lot of factors go into answering that question, but the most important factor is which side is the same-sex parent—Internalizer or Externalizer? The next question is "Do I tend to give-in to my programming, avoid it altogether, or fight it in this case?"

Exercise: If you suspect this is an issue for you, on the continuum below place an X on the line where you estimate that you "default" setting is for Ego-Strength. You may tend to slide up and down depending on the context or situation, put the X where you tend to be most often or on average.

Low Ego Strength		Rigid Ego Strength

If this is or was an issue for you, explore how so and identify which of the Drivers and Mini-Scripts may be active in driving your behavior. Do you tend to fight the script you were given, avoid it altogether, or do you tend to give-in to it? Which "Allowers" do you need to employ here? Finally, if it was an issue for either of them, answer these same questions as it relates to each of your parents.

_____
_____
_____
_____
_____
_____
_____
_____
_____
_____
_____
_____
_____
_____
_____
_____
_____

2.6.3 Boundary Scripting:

The energy from the **Vulnerable Child** ego-state helps us to let our guard down and **CONNECT** with others. The energy from our angry/Defiant Child helps us **SEPARATE** from others. It helps us say "No." When we discount and disown our Angry/Defiant energy our Vulnerable/Needy energy tends to magnify. This is a set-up to have problems saying no—i.e., set and reinforce a boundary.

Our own **Boundaries** are heavily influenced by the parenting we received. Frequently in dysfunctional families one parent is a dominant, demanding and rigid Externalizer while the other is submissive, surrendering, Internalizer with low self-esteem. This leaves our Little Professor with a choice—which do I want to be? A lot of factors go into answering that question, but the most important factor is which side is the same-sex parent—weak boundaries or rigid boundaries? The next question is "Do I tend to give-in to my programming, avoid it altogether, or fight it in this case?"

Exercise: If you suspect this is an issue for you, on the continuum below place an X on the line where you estimate that you "default" setting is for Boundaries. You may tend to slide up and down depending on the context or situation, put the X where you tend to be most often or on average.

| Absent/weak Boundaries | | Rigid Boundaries |

If this is or was an issue for you, explore how so and identify which of the Drivers and Mini-Scripts may be active in driving your behavior. Do you tend to fight the script you were given, avoid it altogether, or do you tend to give-in to it? Which "Allowers" do you need to employ here? Finally, if it was an issue for either of them, answer these same questions as it relates to each of your parents.

_____

_____

_____

_____

2.6.4 Attachment Scripting:

The energy from the **Vulnerable Child** ego-state helps us to **CONNECT** with others. The energy from our angry/Defiant Child helps us to **SEPARATE** from others. When we discount and disown our Angry/Defiant energy our Vulnerable/Needy energy tends to magnify. When we discount and disown our Vulnerable/Needy energy our Angry/Defiant energy tends to magnify. This is a set-up to have attachment issues.

Our ability to attach to others is heavily influenced by the parenting we received. Frequently in dysfunctional families one parent is a dominant, distancing Externalizer with a fear of being trapped, while the other is a submissive, pursuing Internalizer with a terror of abandonment. This set up leaves our little professor with a choice—which do I want to be? A lot of factors go into answering that question, but the most important factor is which side is the same-sex parent—Internalizer or Externalizer? The next question is "Do I tend to give-in to my programming, avoid it altogether, or fight it in this case?"

Exercise: If you suspect this is an issue for you, on the continuum below place an X on the line where you estimate that you "default" setting is for Attachment issues. You may tend to slide up and down depending on the context or situation, put the X where you tend to be most often or on average.

Fear of Abandonment		Fear of Being Trapped

If this is or was an issue for you, explore how so and identify which of the Drivers and Mini-Scripts may be active in driving your behavior. Do you tend to fight the script you were given, avoid it altogether, or do you tend to give-in to it? Which "Allowers" do you need to employ here? Finally, if it was an issue for either of them, answer these same questions as it relates to each of your parents.

2.6.5 Mistrust Scripting:

Our **ability to trust** others is heavily influenced by the parenting we received. Sometimes in dysfunctional families one parent is a dominant, demanding and abusive Externalizer while the other is submissive, surrendering, abused Internalizer with low ego-strength. There may be alcoholism or other active addiction in the family where chaos, broken promises and danger were the norm.

When safety needs are at stake trust is almost impossible to come by. The Little Professor tends to employ repetition compulsion by using naïveté and gullibility (discounting "red flags"), perhaps to stay "in practice" and be prepared, or reaction formation by being Hypervigilant and distrusting as a means of protection. The main question is "Do I tend to give-in to my programming (repetition compulsion), avoid it altogether, or fight it (reaction formation) in this case?"

Exercise: If you suspect this is an issue for you, on the continuum below place an X on the line where you estimate that you "default" setting is for Mistrust. You may tend to slide up and down depending on the context or situation, put the X where you tend to be most often or on average.

| Hypovigilance, Naïve/Gullible | Hypervigilance, Distrusting |

If this is or was an issue for you, explore how so and identify which of the Drivers and Mini-Scripts may be active in driving your behavior. Do you tend to fight the script you were given, avoid it altogether, or do you tend to give-in to it? Which "Allowers" do you need to employ here? Finally, if it was an issue for either of them, answer these same questions as it relates to each of your parents.

_____
_____
_____
_____
_____
_____
_____
_____
_____
_____
_____
_____
_____
_____
_____
_____
_____
_____
_____

2.6.7 Dependence Scripting:

Our **dependence on others** is heavily influenced by the parenting we received. Frequently in dysfunctional families one parent is a dominant, demanding and anti-dependent Externalizer (*"I don't need you—I don't need anybody!"*) while the other is a submissive, surrendering, and dependent Internalizer with low self-worth.

When we discount and disown our Angry/Defiant energy, our Vulnerable/Needy energy tends to magnify. When we discount and disown our Vulnerable/Needy energy, our Angry/Defiant energy tends to magnify. This is a set up to have attachment issues, leaving our Little Professor with a choice—which do I want to be? A lot of factors go into answering that question, but the most important factor is which side is the same-sex parent—Internalizer or Externalizer? The next question is "Do I tend to give-in to my programming, avoid it altogether, or fight it in this case?"

Exercise: If you suspect this is an issue for you, on the continuum below, place an X on the line where you estimate that you "default" setting is for Dependence on others. You may tend to slide up and down depending on the context or situation, put the X where you tend to be most often or on average.

Needy & Dependent		Needless & Anti-Dependent

If this is or was an issue for you, explore how so and identify which of the Drivers and Mini-Scripts may be active in driving your behavior. Do you tend to fight the script you were given, avoid it altogether, or do you tend to give-in to it? Which "Allowers" do you need to employ here? Finally, if it was an issue for either of them, answer these same questions as it relates to each of your parents.

2.6.8 Impulse Control Scripting:

The **ability to control our impulses** is heavily influenced by the parenting we received—especially in the area of discipline. Good discipline is firm, effective and consistent; if we were not held accountable by a permissive parent then we may not have developed the internal structures to control our impulses very well. If our parent was overly strict, hard to please, or had an *"Automatic No"* response, we may have learned to rigidly control our impulses. We may have rarely acted out or may have even become fearful of being spontaneous.

Frequently in dysfunctional families there is a lot of chaos and unpredictability in the home. Kids are like a barometer for such things; when things are not right at home kids tend to act-out and misbehave. Some refer to behavior like this as "… bouncing off the walls." Sadly, sometimes the misbehavior is mistaken for ADHD or Mania and the child is put on medicine. The main question is "Do I tend to give-in to my programming, avoid it altogether, or fight it in this case?"

Exercise: If you suspect this is an issue for you, on the continuum below, place an X on the line where you estimate that you "default" setting is for Impulse Control. You may tend to slide up and down depending on the context or situation, put the X where you tend to be most often or on average.

| Poor Impulse Control | Rigid Impulse Control |

If this is or was an issue for you, explore how so and identify which of the Drivers and Mini-Scripts may be active in driving your behavior. Do you tend to fight the script you were given, avoid it altogether, or do you tend to give-in to it? Which "Allowers" do you need to employ here? Finally, if it was an issue for either of them, answer these same questions as it relates to each of your parents.

_____

_____

_____

_____

_____

_____

_____

_____

_____

_____

_____

_____

_____

_____

_____

_____

_____

_____

_____

2.6.9 Emotional Regulation Scripting:

When children are **subjected to constant stress** and not enough time, attention, or affection they may have trouble soothing themselves. In less-than-nurturing families there is frequently a high level of ongoing stress due to whatever the dysfunction is. Good parenting requires the ability to nurture and care for the child. This function of parenting helps the child experience soothing from the outside which is integrated by the Little Professor on the inside as strategies to self-soothe are devised.

When soothing doesn't come or is not available the child may experience constant over-stimulation resulting in emotional over-reactivity, or emotional numbness due to what Terrence Gorski calls the "Circuit Breaker effect"—when over-stimulation becomes unbearable the emotional circuits may simply shut down. Emotional cutoff is the term for constantly unemotional persons. In TA they call it being "stuck in the Adult ego-state," which is likened to a computer, and excluding the Child-created ego-states from awareness. Emotional over-reaction may come from the Vulnerable/Needy part (depression) or the Angry/Defiant part (anger problems). It could even be a problem with all Child-created parts across the board. The main question is "Do I tend to give-in to my programming, avoid it altogether, or fight it in this case?"

Exercise: If you suspect this is an issue for you, on the continuum below place an X on the line where you estimate that you "default" setting is for Emotional Regulation. You may tend to slide up and down depending on the context or situation, put the X where you tend to be most often or on average.

| Emotional Over-Reactivity | | Emotional Numbness |

If this is or was an issue for you, explore how so and identify which of the Drivers and Mini-Scripts may be active in driving your behavior. Do you tend to fight the script you were given, avoid it altogether, or do you tend to give-in to it? Which "Allowers" do you need to employ here? Finally, if it was an issue for either of them, answer these same questions as it relates to each of your parents.

_____

_____

_____

_____

_____

_____

_____

_____

_____

_____

_____

_____

_____

2.7 Shame-Based Script Elements

2.7.1 Shame Scripting:

The level of Toxic shame we carry is heavily influenced by the parenting we received. In fact, in his video *Shame and Addiction*, John Bradshaw said that ninety percent of our shame is transferred to us from the previous generation.

Frequently in dysfunctional families one parent is a dominant, demanding and *shameless* Externalizer while the other is a submissive, surrendering, and *shameful* Internalizer. Both parents pass on their shame through modeling and/or direct statements of their own wounded Inner Children—whether it's from the Vulnerable/Needy Child in the parent saying such things as *"Look at what you're doing to me!"* or the Angry/Defiant Child in the parent acting out their anger by physical abuse. Most often it is the shaming messages of the Critical Parent in the parent that does the most harm (i.e., belittling and name-calling) as its messages are recorded in the Critical Parent ego-state in the child. The question is "Do I tend to give-in to my programming, avoid it altogether, or fight it in this case?"

Exercise: If you suspect this is an issue for you, on the continuum below place an X on the line where you estimate that you "default" setting is for Shame. You may tend to slide up and down depending on the context or situation, put the X where you tend to be most often or on average.

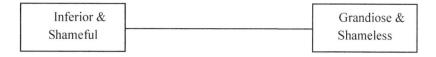

| Inferior & Shameful | | Grandiose & Shameless |

If this is or was an issue for you, explore how so and identify which of the Drivers and Mini-Scripts may be active in driving your behavior. Do you tend to fight the script you were given, avoid it altogether, or do you tend to give-in to it? Which "Allowers" do you need to employ here? Finally, if it was an issue for either of them, answer these same questions as it relates to each of your parents.

_____

_____

_____

_____

_____

_____

_____

_____

_____

_____

_____

_____

_____

_____

_____

_____

2.7.2 Performance Scripting:

Our **ability to perform comfortably** is heavily influenced by the parenting we received. Frequently in dysfunctional families one or both parents give their approval only when the child performs well at something. This performance related approval can lead to a fear of failure because the cost is so high. Other times parents tend to discourage their kids by not rewarding them for good performance. In fact, sometimes an Internalizing parent may send a *"don't do better than me"* injunction by saying things like, *"that's nice dear,* (sigh) *I wish I could have had an opportunity like that when I was your age"* to a child who excels on a school project.

Often in a less-than-nurturing family, an Externalizing parent displays grandiose, self-aggrandizing behavior by frequently bragging about their accomplishments and how they know more than all those other stupid people in the world. This can be very unattractive to a child who may link success with grandiosity, thereby becoming afraid to succeed for fear of becoming like the self-aggrandizing parent. This leaves our Little Professor with a choice—which do I want to be? A lot of factors go into answering that question, but the most important factor is which side is the same-sex parent—Internalizer or Externalizer? The next question is "Do I tend to give-in to my programming, avoid it altogether, or fight it in this case?"

Exercise: If you suspect this is an issue for you, on the continuum below place an X on the line where you estimate that you "default" setting is for Performance. You may tend to slide up and down depending on the context or situation, put the X where you tend to be most often or on average

Fear of Success		Fear of Failure

If this is or was an issue for you, explore how so and identify which of the Drivers and Mini-Scripts may be active in driving your behavior. Do you tend to fight the script you were given, avoid it altogether, or do you tend to give-in to it? Which "Allowers" do you need to employ here? Finally, if it was an issue for either of them, answer these same questions as it relates to each of your parents.

_____

_____

_____

_____

_____

_____

_____

_____

2.7.3 Criticism Scripting:

There are **two kinds of criticism**, the kind that's **meant to help** and the kind that's **meant to hurt**. But in a dysfunctional family the kind that's meant to help is also meant to hurt. The positive intention of a shame-based critical parent is to help, but they do it in the way it was passed on to them—through the shaming messages of a Critical Parent. A parent usually demonstrates the kind of Parenting they received as a child.

Our ability to tolerate criticism is heavily influenced by the parenting we received. Frequently in dysfunctional families one parent is a dominant, demanding and outwardly critical Externalizer while the other is submissive, surrendering, inwardly critical Internalizer with low, low-self-esteem. This set up leaves our little professor with a choice—which do I want to be? A lot of factors go into answering that question, but the most important factor is which side is the same-sex parent—Internalizer or Externalizer? The next question is "Do I tend to give-in to my programming, avoid it altogether, or fight it in this case?"

Exercise: If you suspect this is an issue for you, on the continuum below place an X on the line where you estimate that you "default" setting is for Criticism. You may tend to slide up and down depending on the context or situation, put the X where you tend to be most often or on average.

Hypersensitive to Criticism		Hypercritical of Self/Others

If this is or was an issue for you, explore how so and identify which of the Drivers and Mini-Scripts may be active in driving your behavior. Do you tend to fight the script you were given, avoid it altogether, or do you tend to give-in to it? Which "Allowers" do you need to employ here? Finally, if it was an issue for either of them, answer these same questions as it relates to each of your parents.

_____

_____

_____

_____

_____

_____

_____

_____

_____

_____

_____

_____

_____

_____

_____

_____

2.7.4 Achievement Scripting:

Our level of Achievement is directly tied to one's Ego-Strength which is defined above as "… the ability to maintain the ego by a cluster of traits that together contributes to good mental health. The traits usually considered important include tolerance of the pain of loss, disappointment, shame, or guilt; forgiveness of those who have caused an injury, with feelings of compassion rather than anger and retaliation; acceptance of substitutes and ability to defer gratification; persistence and perseverance in the pursuit of goals; openness, flexibility, and creativity in learning to adapt; and vitality and power in the activities of life."

Our level of achievement is heavily influenced by the parenting we received. Frequently in dysfunctional families one parent is a dominant, demanding Externalizer with rigid ego-strength while the other is a submissive, surrendering, perfectionistic Internalizer with low ego-strength. Perfectionism can be an overcompensation for fear of failure also referred to "a desire to be beyond criticism" because with low ego-strength any criticism can be devastating. The question is "Do I tend to give-in to my programming, avoid it altogether, or fight it in this case?"

Exercise: If you suspect this is an issue for you, on the continuum below place an X on the line where you estimate that you "default" setting is for Achievement. You may tend to slide up and down depending on the context or situation, put the X where you tend to be most often or on average.

Under-Achievement		Perfectionism

If this is or was an issue for you, explore how so and identify which of the Drivers and Mini-Scripts may be active in driving your behavior. Do you tend to fight the script you were given, avoid it altogether, or do you tend to give-in to it? Which "Allowers" do you need to employ here? Finally, if it was an issue for either of them, answer these same questions as it relates to each of your parents.

_____

_____

_____

_____

_____

_____

_____

_____

_____

_____

_____

_____

_____

_____

2.8 Contempt-Based Script Elements

2.8.1 Hopefulness Scripting:

Frequently in less-than-nurturing families a child has her **hope dashed** over and over again by broken promises and chaos in the home. Frequently in less-than-nurturing families a child has her **hopes dashed** over and over by broken promises due to chaos in the home. She discovers the one thing she can count on is being let down. Couple this with the criticalness of a shame-based family system and one can quite easily develop a habit of pessimism and negativity. Hope becomes a dangerous thing to children in this situation because they can get hurt more by hoping than by being cynical.

Our level of hopefulness is heavily influenced by the parenting we received. Frequently in dysfunctional families, one parent is an outwardly pessimistic, punitive, and negative Externalizer while the other is an inwardly pessimistic, negative and controlling Internalizer (Sometimes they briefly switch roles). The main question is "do I tend to give-in to my programming, avoid it altogether, or fight it in this case?" Unrealistic Optimism can be an overcompensation (reaction formation) to fight against a pessimism script element. Or it could be part of a survival role assignment of Mascot which may include a "Please Others with a happy bubble" driver.

Exercise: If you suspect this is an issue for you, on the continuum below place an X on the line where you estimate that you "default" setting is for Hopefulness. You may tend to slide up and down depending on the context or situation, put the X where you tend to be most often or on average.

Pessimism & Negativity at Self or Others		Unrealistic Optimism at Self or Others

If this is or was an issue for you, explore how so and identify which of the Drivers and Mini-Scripts may be active in driving

your behavior. Do you tend to fight the script you were given, avoid it altogether, or do you tend to give-in to it? Which "Allowers" do you need to employ here? Finally, if it was an issue for either of them, answer these same questions as it relates to each of your parents.

_____
_____
_____
_____
_____
_____
_____
_____
_____
_____
_____
_____

2.8.2 Blame Scripting:

Frequently in a less-than-nurturing family someone must carry the **blame** for whatever is going wrong at any given time. When blame is assigned then all of ones unfinished anger can have a place to go. And in a dysfunctional family there is no shortage of unfinished business in the form of anger, resentment, and frustration.

Frequently one parent is a dominant, demanding and punitive Externalizer who assigns blame while the other is submissive, surrendering, self-deprecating Internalizer who accepts blame. When the Internalizer directs the anger inward at self it becomes depression and "shame attacks." Externalizing anger requires being able to make one's self really believe it's the other person(s) fault—leading to "rage attacks." This set up leaves our little professor with a choice— which do I want to be? A lot of factors go into answering that question, but the most important factor is which side is the same-sex parent—Internalizer or Externalizer? The next question is "Do I tend to give-in to my programming, avoid it altogether, or fight it in this case?"

Exercise: If you suspect this is an issue for you, on the continuum below place an X on the line where you estimate that you "default" setting is for Blame. You may tend to slide up and down depending on the context or situation, put the X where you tend to be most often or on average.

Internalized Anger/Depression		Externalized Anger/Rage

If this is or was an issue for you, explore how so and identify which of the Drivers and Mini-Scripts may be active in driving your behavior. Do you tend to fight the script you were given, avoid it altogether, or do you tend to give-in to it? Which "Allowers" do you need to employ here? Finally, if it was an issue for either of them, answer these same questions as it relates to each of your parents.

_____
_____
_____
_____
_____
_____
_____
_____
_____
_____
_____
_____
_____
_____

2.8.3 Communication Style Scripting:

There are three basic styles of **communication: Passive, Assertive,** and **Aggressive**. With Passive communication the person does nothing to protect themselves (discounting their Angry/Defiant part) and the Aggressive style the person defends their own rights without regard for the other person(s) (discounting the empathy of their Vulnerable Child ego-state). The Assertive style of communication is the healthiest because it doesn't discount anything—Assertiveness is about defending one's own rights while respecting the rights of the other(s) involved.

Our own communication style is heavily influenced by the parenting we received. Frequently in dysfunctional families one parent is an aggressive, demanding and rigid Externalizer while the other is a passive, surrendering, Internalizer with low ego-strength (and sometimes they briefly switch roles). This set-up leaves our little professor with a choice—which do I want to be? A lot of factors go into answering that question, but the most important factor is which side is the same-sex parent—Internalizer or Externalizer? The next question is "Do I tend to give-in to my programming, avoid it altogether, or fight it in this case?"

Exercise: If you suspect this is an issue for you, on the continuum below place an X on the line where you estimate that you "default" setting is for Communication Style. You may tend to slide up and down depending on the context or situation, put the X where you tend to be most often or on average.

If this is or was an issue for you, explore how so and identify which of the Drivers & Mini-Scripts may be active in driving your behavior. Do you tend to fight the script you were given, avoid it altogether, or do you tend to give-in to it? Which "Allowers" do you need to employ here? Finally, if it was an issue for either of them, answer these same questions as it relates to each of your parents.

_____

_____

_____

_____

_____

_____

_____

_____

_____

_____

_____

_____

_____

_____

2.8.4 Expectation/Entitlement Scripting:

Many times discouragement comes to us because we have unrealistic expectations about how things are "supposed" to turn out. The fallacy of fairness is frequently behind this. I suspect that the first sentence a child learns to speak is most often *"That's not fair!"* We go through life using that argument until we learn that "life" and "the world" is not always "fair." It is magical thinking to assume that everything "should" work out the way we want them to every time.

When parents operate from their own Life Script, whether they tend to Internalize or Externalize their abandonment, shame and contempt, they are in their Child created ego-states. The Child created ego-states use the magical thinking of childhood rather than the objective cause-and-effect thinking of the Adult ego-state. If I have a script element where I expect everything to go my way (or "I want what I want when I want it!"), I need to ask myself "do I tend to give-in to my programming, avoid it altogether, or fight it in this case? With the defense of reaction formation (aka; a *Little Professor* Strategy) I might *expect nothing* to go my way and unleash my punitive Critical Parent message inward to beat Vulnerable Child up for even hoping it might be different this time!

Exercise: If you suspect this is an issue for you, on the continuum below place an X on the line where you estimate that you "default" setting is for Expectation. You may tend to slide up and down depending on the context or situation, put the X where you tend to be most often or on average.

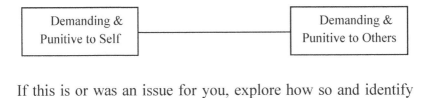

| Demanding & Punitive to Self | | Demanding & Punitive to Others |

If this is or was an issue for you, explore how so and identify which of the Drivers & Mini-Scripts may be active in driving your behavior. Do you tend to fight the script you were given, avoid it altogether, or do you tend to give-in to it? Which "Allowers" do you need to employ here? Finally, if it was an issue for either of them, answer these same questions as it relates to each of your parents.

_____
_____
_____
_____
_____
_____
_____
_____
_____
_____
_____
_____

2.9 External Focus-Based Script Elements

2.9.1 Focus of Attention Scripting:

Those who tend to be primarily Internalizers are "Other-Centered"—due to their need for an external focus to avoid what is going on internally, Internalizers subconsciously seek out and find problem partners. What better way to keep your focus outward than to be unequally yoked to a problem person? Externalizers tend to focus their attention primarily on themselves. This is a complimentary arrangement; if I am an Externalizer then I am *"all-about-me"* and my Internalizing partner is *"all-about-me-too."*

Frequently in dysfunctional families one parent is a dominant, demanding and self-centered Externalizer while the other is submissive, surrendering, other-centered Internalizer with low ego-strength (and sometimes they briefly switch roles). This set up leaves our little professor with a choice—which do I want to be? A lot of factors go into answering that question, but the most important factor is which side is the same-sex parent—Internalizer or Externalizer? The next question is "Do I tend to give-in to my programming, avoid it altogether, or fight it in this case?"

Exercise: If you suspect this is an issue for you, on the continuum below place an X on the line where you estimate that you "dcfault" setting for where you direct you attention. You may tend to slide up and down depending on the context or situation, put the X where you tend to be most often or on average.

Other Centered		Self Absorbed

If this is or was an issue for you, explore how so and identify which of the Drivers and Mini-Scripts may be active in driving your behavior. Do you tend to fight the script you were given, avoid it altogether, or do you tend to give-in to it? Which "Allowers" do you need to employ here? Finally, if it was an issue for either of them, answer these same questions as it relates to each of your parents.

_____

_____

_____

_____

_____

_____

_____

_____

_____

_____

_____

_____

_____

_____

2.9.2 Involvement Scripting:

Keeping an external focus requires a distraction. If I have no distraction then my focus begins to drift inward. As that occurs, I become aware of anxiety which is the precursor to the surfacing of the emotional pain I have been "stuffing" inside.

For Codependents, ("Professional Internalizers") a lot of distraction is required; so much so that they subconsciously involve themselves in as many activities as it takes to make sure they have ABSOLUTELY no time for themselves. They also addictively involve themselves with a problem partner with whom they can obsess over while they are carrying out all of the community and after school responsibilities they have signed up for over the years—they become a "Human Doing." In addition to their many other duties, the Codependent Internalizer is frequently addicted to the addict and they obsess over their addict. Externalizers tend to involve themselves in relationships with objects and events and don't seem to care much about life and People—in other words, they develop addictions, obsessions, and compulsions to keep themselves medicated and distracted. The main question is "Do I tend to give-in to my programming, avoid it altogether, or fight it in this case?"

Exercise: If you suspect this is an issue for you, on the continuum below place an X on the line where you estimate that you "default" setting is for Involvement. You may tend to slide up and down depending on the context or situation, put the X where you tend to be most often or on average.

Over-involved		Apathetic & Uninvolved

If this is or was an issue for you, explore how so and identify which of the Drivers and Mini-Scripts may be active in driving your behavior. Do you tend to fight the script you were given, avoid it altogether, or do you tend to give-in to it? Which "Allowers" do you need to employ here? Finally, if it was an issue for either of them, answer these same questions as it relates to each of your parents.

_____
_____
_____
_____
_____
_____
_____
_____
_____
_____
_____
_____
_____
_____

2.10 Invented Self-Based Script Elements

2.10.1 Praise Scripting:

Internalizers and Externalizers alike tend to seek attention and recognition although many times most of them cannot really accept it when they get it. The mask of the Invented self is a public image that is projected to the world for just that purpose—to find approval and acceptance from others. Since we cannot "go inside" to find comfort and relief, we have to look toward outer sources for it. The problem come when we discover that for some unknown reason the praise we get does not feel quite right—it is usually because deep down (in our False Self) we feel like a phony, "If they really knew me they wouldn't be saying those nice things about me."

Frequently in dysfunctional families one parent is a dominant, demanding and self-centered Externalizer. This parent may actually feel pretty good when getting the recognition and attention they seek. This is because they are a lot more out-of-touch with their inner world. Internalizers may not be able to genuine accept praise, but they sure can feel it when someone important to them gets upset or disappointed in them. This is covered in the material on Impression Management. The main question is "Do I tend to give-in to my programming, avoid it altogether, or fight it in this case?"

Exercise: If you suspect this is an issue for you, on the continuum below place an X on the line where you estimate that you "default" setting is for Praise. You may tend to slide up and down depending on the context or situation, put the X where you tend to be most often or on average.

| Seeking Attention | | Avoids Attention & |

If this is or was an issue for you, explore how so and identify which of the Drivers and Mini-Scripts may be active in driving

your behavior. Do you tend to fight the script you were given, avoid it altogether, or do you tend to give-in to it? Which "Allowers" do you need to employ here? Finally, if it was an issue for either of them, answer these same questions as it relates to each of your parents.

_____

_____

_____

_____

_____

_____

_____

_____

_____

_____

_____

_____

_____

_____

2.10.2 Self-Value Scripting:

Because we carry the pain of abandonment, shame, and contempt, our self-value is not too high. Growing up in a shame-based family system doesn't help much either. The very nature of the False-Self makes it hard to value ourselves. This is why many times you will hear self-depreciating comments from children of dysfunctional backgrounds.

Our own Self-Value is heavily influenced by the parenting we received. If I tend to lean toward the Internalizer side of the continuum I am more likely to be self-depreciating. Externalizers tend to gravitate toward the Self-Aggrandizing side. Grandiosity and self-aggrandizing are overcompensations or reaction formations to the feelings of low self-worth. In order to recovery from any of the wounds and script elements outlined herein, The Externalizer must eventually get in touch with the pain that has been distorted by reaction formation and repression. The main question is "Do I tend to give-in to my programming, avoid it altogether, or fight it in this case?"

Exercise: If you suspect this is an issue for you, on the continuum below place an X on the line where you estimate that you "default" setting is for Self-Value. You may tend to slide up and down depending on the context or situation, put the X where you tend to be most often or on average.

Self-Depreciating		Self-Aggrandizing

If this is or was an issue for you, explore how so and identify which of the Drivers and Mini-Scripts may be active in driving your behavior. Do you tend to fight the script you were given, avoid it altogether, or do you tend to give-in to it? Which "Allowers" do you need to employ here? Finally, if it was an issue for either of them, answer these same questions as it relates to each of your parents.

_____

_____

_____

_____

_____

_____

_____

_____

_____

_____

_____

_____

_____

_____

_____

_____

_____

_____

_____

_____

2.11 TA Frame of Reference and Redefining Reality

Each day of our lives, from the moment we awaken in the morning until the time we go back to sleep at night we are continually faced with opportunities to make decisions, solve problems, learn something new, interact with others, and get things done. In Transactional Analysis, how effectively we handle or don't handle these opportunities depends upon our choice of two frames of reference: We can choose to operate consciously from the full power of our purposeful, resourceful, here-and-now focused Adult ego-state or *we can go into subconscious "auto-pilot" and operate from within our Life Script.* We refer to the latter as "Going into Script."

Our Life Script is programmed into us—we don't have to remember to do it and, therefore, we don't have to apply any energy or concentration either! In fact, it is actually EASIER to operate from within our script! The Life Script frame of reference is part of us; it is actually encoded into our neural circuitry. The other frame of reference, behaving *autonomously of our script*, requires that we apply conscious effort to stay in the "here-and-now" rather than being triggered or "rubberbanded" back into the "there-and-then." It requires that we stay fully aware and in charge of all of our ego-states and Adult resources.

Because it takes so much energy and effort to concentrate on staying autonomous, many of us frequently take little or no action even when we know what we need to do—that's how we stay stuck. And we can only explain our inaction as due to some magical force over which we have little or no control. It is usually when we reach the threshold of our tolerance for pain (aka, Hitting Bottom) that we choose to begin taking action—even then it can be very difficult to *stay out of our script* at times.

2.11.1 Discounting and Grandiosity

When we "go into script" we necessarily have to discount, delete and/or distort some portion of reality. We have to subconsciously ignore relevant information in order to play out our mini-script processes. For example, let's say I go to a restaurant and order my favorite meal and have been looking forward to it all week. The waitress tells me they are out of that dish for the rest of the week. I feel very disappointed and say to my Self *"Why does this ALWAYS have to happen to me. When I want something I can NEVER have it!"* I then tense up my jaw, make my face red, snap at the waitress, and walk out of the restaurant in a tiff.

In order to play out the "Always" and "Never" mini-scripts I had to discount my Adult cause-and-effect thinking and lapse into the magical thinking of childhood. Otherwise I would have maintained my composure long enough to remind myself that I got many things I wanted that very day. I drove my car to the restaurant, I had the money to buy my meal, I have even wanted and eaten that very same meal many times in the past. And, if I could wait just a few days, I would be able to enjoy my favorite dish once it becomes available again.

Every time we discount some portion of reality, another portion of reality gets magnified. This is referred to in TA as grandiosity. This is how things "get blown out of proportion" and how "molehills" become "mountains." In the example above, beneath my awareness, I *discounted* my Adult cause-and-effect reasoning and *magnified* my magical child-like thinking to the extent that it became very powerful and took control. The Angry/Defiant child ego-state was "driving my bus" at that moment. Later, after I calmed down and "thought" about it while from my autonomous Adult ego-state, I would likely have felt embarrassed about my angry tirade. "Things" would have returned to their rightful proportion.

Here's another example of discounting and grandiosity: Let's say I am almost hit by a careless driver who barged right out in front of me, cutting me off in a close call. I become enraged and make rude gestures as I tailgate him for the next few blocks. I am so furious that I miss the red light and barge right through the intersection causing a near collision with another driver. I *now* become enraged because there is a man tailgating me and making rude gestures!

Exercise: How many discounts (*ignoring of reality*) and examples of grandiosity (*magnifications of reality*) can you find in the above example?

_____

_____

_____

_____

_____

_____

_____

_____

_____

_____

_____

_____

_____

Can you give an example of a recent triggering situation when you discounted, deleted or ignored important information and distorted another feature of that same situation by "blowing it out of proportion"?

_____

_____

_____

_____

_____

_____

_____

_____

_____

2.11.2 My Map of the World

Before we give up the excessive need for control, take off the mask, and turn our focus inward, we need to understand a little more about how we subconsciously get caught up in certain dysfunctional patterns and relationships by redefining, deleting, and distorting. In order to do that we need to explore some basics about how the human brain processes information.

Human beings are meaning-makers. We have to make sense out of the things that happen around us and to us. To accomplish this, the first thing we must be able to do is to take in raw sensory data from *"the World"* around us. Unless we are sensory impaired or challenged in a particular area, there are five input channels we use to receive *sensory data* from the world. They are the *visual (sight), auditory (sound), kinesthetic (touch), olfactory (smell), and gustatory (taste)* input channels. (See Meta Map below)

2.11.3 Inputting Sensory Data

At any given moment, there is somewhere in the neighborhood of two million bits of sensory data coming in from the world through our input channels. The subconscious mind can handle only about forty thousand bits of incoming data per second. Therefore, incoming data must be sorted into two categories; relevant data and irrelevant data. The relevant data is allowed in and the irrelevant data is deleted—the proverbial *"in one ear and out the other."*

The screening and sorting processes are completed by the thalamus and the reticular activating system (RAS). Fortunately, it's not important to remember these two structures or to know exactly how they work for our purposes here. However, a good way to think about it is to imagine that there is *a doorman to the unconscious mind* called the reticular activating system (RAS). Below is *a map of how our mind makes maps* of "reality"—a Meta-Map. (See below)

It is the "doorman's" responsibility to allow entry to those bits of hear-see-feel data that are important to me and delete, or screen out those data which are not relevant. So, how does the doorman know which data is important to me? There are several primary *mental or perceptual filters* that tell the doorman to the subconscious mind what data is relevant. They are:

- Identity
- Values
- Strongly-held beliefs
- Memories and experiences
- Programs
- Survival needs

Based upon these mental filters, the RAS, in communication with the thalamus and pre-frontal cortex, uses three universal processes; *Generalization, Deletion, and Distortion* to complete the screening and sorting function.

My Map of the World

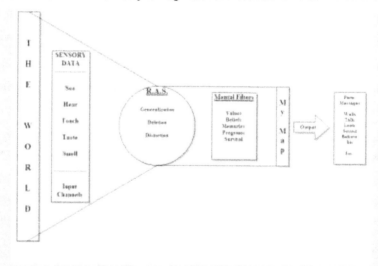

Meta-Map

Here is an example of how it works:

John comes in for his first counseling session. He states his main concern is his strongly held belief that he is *not worth caring about*. The counselor notices that John has been married for fifteen years. He asks, *"What about your wife, doesn't she care about you?"* John says, *"No, she doesn't care about me and ever since I can remember no one has ever cared about me. I've resigned myself to the fact that I'm just not worth caring about."*

The counselor has trouble accepting this, so he asks John, *"I'd like to come and stay at your house this weekend just to observe. I'd like to see for myself if your wife really doesn't care about you—would that be alright?"* John agrees to allow this and the weekend comes and goes.

The counselor and John meet in session the following week. The counselor opens by saying, *"John, I counted a total of 63 caring messages from your wife to you over the weekend."* John replies, *"What are you talking about? I didn't hear even one caring comment."* The counselor played a tape recording from a hand-held tape recorder that he carried with him over the weekend. Sure enough, there were 63 messages that could be considered caring from John's wife. John systematically discounts each one, *"Oh, she just wanted something,"* *"She was just trying to look good for you,"* *"She didn't really mean it,"* and *"She was just saying that because ..."*

The generalization was John's strongly held belief–*"I'm not worth caring about."* Any incoming sensory data (*visual, auditory, or kinesthetic* caring messages) that did not support the belief were deleted (discounted). They just didn't register with John and instead went *"in one ear and out the other."* When John couldn't delete the messages on the tape recording, his "doorman" distorted (discounted) them for him with defense mechanisms such as *magnification, rationalization, minimization, intellectualization, and denial.* The result was that his subconscious mind helped John sort for only the data that would support his strongly held belief that he isn't worth caring about.

John's strongly-held belief is rooted in subconscious primary Injunctions (*Don't Exist & Don't be Important*). He is even partly aware of this when he says he can trace the evidence of the belief back to the things his Externalizing father told him about his value AND worth. John disconnects from the obvious–that his belief is the result of his father's statements, not evidence of it. Accepting his father's injunctions "scripted" John's Self-Value so that his "doorman" allowed in only the data that supported the belief, thereby reinforcing and strengthening the belief.

Every time he "finds" more "evidence" of it, John re-experiences the emotional charge that came with the confirmation of his psychological position that he is "NOT Okay." This not only strengthens of the belief, it *magnifies the magical thinking and emotional re-experiencing of his wounded Vulnerable Child energy of the past*. At a deeper level, beneath the waterline of our conscious awareness, the re-living of this original imprint experience reinforces and strengthens the Injunction & Counter Injunction: *"I can exist, so long as I accept my unimportance and lack of worth to others."* I may only be aware of feeling "Not worth caring about" (i.e., NOT Okay).

2.11.4 Mind-Movies & Data Processing

Once the data that did support John's *mental filters* made it past the doorman (RAS) and into the subconscious mind, the *thalamus* then sorts and packages the raw hear-see-feel data into a coherent form. A good analogy is to think of it as producing a movie in the mind. This *mind-movie* has a visual track, a soundtrack, a touch track, and sometimes a smell track and taste track. Organizing the data into a movie form allows us to step back and *re-present* to ourselves *"what just happened"* so we can interpret it and assign meaning to it that fits our experience. This is why sensory input channels are referred to as representational systems in the field of Neuro Linguistic Programming (NLP).

Key Point: *The sensory data we use to produce these mind-movies are incomplete, biased, and skewed data* as in the example above. That is, they are *filtered* data that support our present mental filters regarding our *identity, values, beliefs, experiences, programs, and survival needs.* In other words, *unless we consciously exert the effort to be objective and open-minded,* we only let in data to support what we already "know" as "reality." In this way, we create a self-fulfilling prophecy.

How many times have you asked someone how they know something is true only to get a response such as *"It's been my experience"*? People tend to believe what they experience and tend to experience what they believe—according to their Life Script. This filtering of biased data results in strengthening our "scripted" perceptions of reality, also known as *subjective* experience. *Objective* experience would require that we take in and consider all available data—something that human beings cannot do fully and completely because we can only handle about forty-thousand bits of the incoming two-million bits of data per second. So we must delete, distort, and otherwise discount huge portions of what is going on around us–that would be anything that does not fit our Life Script or our "Map of the World."

These automatic mind-movies are usually being viewed just beneath the surface of our awareness by our mind's eye (just about eyebrow level). As we watch these biased re-presentations of *"what just happened"* we have thoughts and feelings about the movie we made and, by doing so, assign *meaning* to the movie. Re-presenting this movie in this fashion is the pre-frontal cortex's (thinking brain) attempt to make sense out of "what just happened." It then searches its huge database for a category of past similar experience with which to compare the new incoming data.

When it finds a "match" the thinking brain sends the movie and the meaning assigned to it on to the limbic system (the feeling brain) where the experience gets emotionally "tagged and experienced" by the amygdala. Then the whole package of experience (the movie, meaning, and emotional tag) is sent off to the hippocampus, another part of the limbic system, where it gets processed and added to the appropriate category (or cognitive map) in the database of long-term memory. The emotional charge that is tagged to a significant emotional experience gets triggered whenever a similar emotional experience occurs, providing confirmation of the psychological position (*"I'm not Okay, you're Okay"*).

The new addition updates the existing cognitive map (neural network) for that category thereby *strengthening the strongly held belief that created it*. The updated cognitive map then sends information back to the thinking brain, which then updates the doorman of our subconscious mind about the increased importance of this belief. The doorman responds by letting in even more *biased* data to support that strengthened belief.

We have beliefs about our identity, beliefs about our values, beliefs about our beliefs, beliefs about our memories AND experiences, beliefs about our mental programs, and beliefs about our survival needs. All of these beliefs are strengthened repeatedly throughout the course of our life by intensity and/or repetition. These strongly held beliefs, or generalizations, originating from our perceptual filters and psychological positions become firmly embedded on the neural networks of long-term memory. They are difficult to change–though not impossible.

2.11.5 Out-Putting Sensory Data

So far we have explored how we make meaning by *inputting and processing sensory data* to create our own individual "map of the world." Our map of the world consists of smaller cognitive maps or script elements (encoded on neural networks) with instructions for how to do relationships, how to cook, how to ride a bike, how to do my job, and how to read; what I can expect from myself, other people, and the world in general; and when to feel Okay or NOT Okay. Armed with all of these script elements I can co-create "the world as I know it" with a compatible partner or partners.

At last count there were approximately seven billion people in the world. How many of those seven billion people do you think have *exactly* the same *values, beliefs, memories and experiences, programs, and survival needs?* That's right—no two people have exactly the same mental filters because no two people grew up taking identical roles in the same family under identical circumstances and having identical experiences each and every day of their lives.

Therefore, no two people see or experience the world exactly the same way. That's why if there are three people witnessing an accident, there are three different reports given about what happened. We can conclude from this that there are at least seven billion "maps of the world." So, who has the correct map? The answer is everyone has the correct map for themselves. And each of us "outputs" that map through verbal messages and nonverbal para-messages (See Meta Map, p. 173.)

Para-messages are nonverbal communications sent through body language, tone of voice, facial expression, etc. Over ninety percent of what we communicate to each other is in the form of para-messages. Let's take our example of John, the person who believes, *"I'm not worth caring about."* **When John walks into a room, he "leaks" that belief out of every pore of his body**–*he walks like it, talks like it, sounds like it, acts like it, sits like it, etc.* Through these non-verbal messages, John is sending thousands of bits of hear-see-feel data out into the world around him, outputting this cognitive map. The other people in that room are unconsciously sorting and sifting through that data *allowing in only the bits and pieces that fit their maps of the world.* If the data John is outputting is not compatible with another person's map it will not be allowed in. If it is compatible, if it does fit the other persons map, then the two will *"hit it off."*

The subconscious mind doesn't miss a thing. Have you ever seen a friend walk into the room and can just tell by looking at him/her that something is wrong? When you ask them, *"What's wrong?"* they may reply, *"Nothing's wrong"* but you can tell that's not true. Some people think of this is being able to sense another person's "aura" while others call it "countenance." We have a conscious connection with others and a subconscious connection that helps us attract and be attracted by others who fit our map of the world. It is like we do subconscious auditions looking for those who know how to dance our dance, especially in the mate selection process.

2.11.6 Do I have a Stamp on My Forehead?

So what are the implications of all this? Perhaps another example will clarify. Let's look at the condition referred to as codependency; when someone has codependency their subconscious doorman (RAS) is *programmed to sort and screen for data that will support their mental filters—* **codependent values, codependent beliefs, codependent memories and experiences, codependent programs, and codependent survival skills**:

- **Values** – Please others, self-sacrifice (Be Strong), be perfect, staying busy (Work Hard)
- **Beliefs** – "I'm not good enough," "others are more important than I am," "I must always please others," "if I say no you will go away and not come back"
- **Memories and Experiences** – abandonment experiences, memories of abuse, shameful experiences, repetition compulsions,
- **Programs** – Here's how to … care-take others, rescue others, control the outcomes, try hard to fix others, (Please Others and Hurry up about it!)
- **Survival Skills** – Injunctions, counter-injunctions, and Script elements, approval seeking, don't feel, don't talk, don't trust, etc.

Now let's say that this person has ended her most recent codependent relationship. Hoping for better luck this time she begins looking for a new partner. She walks into a room full of fifty available men; forty-nine of them are healthy and only one of them is alcoholic. She is bound-and-determined to find Mr. Right this time. Who do you think she ends up with? That's right; she soon finds herself wrapped up with another alcoholic partner. She asks herself, *"Why does this keep happening to me? Do I have a stamp on my forehead, or what?"*

No, she doesn't have a stamp on her forehead; she has radar at the base of her skull, it's called the reticular activating system (RAS). Her subconscious doorman is sifting through two million bits of data per second, *allowing in only that data which fits her codependent map of the world*. It just so happens that a person with a codependent map is extremely compatible with someone who has a map for alcoholism or other similar dysfunction. So, he is as drawn to her as she is to him–and so the sparks fly!

Section 3: Getting to know your "True Self"

If I accept that the **False Self** is not really who I am, and the Invented Self is not really who I am, then I must ask: *"Who am I?"*

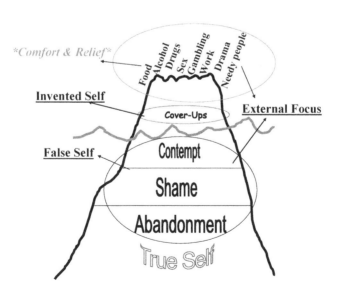

The issues outlined in this book are non-discriminatory. The effects of abandonment, shame and contempt cut across all socio-economic, cultural, racial, political, and other demographic lines–including religious faith. This is because kids are kids no matter where you go; they have the same needs across the globe. 12-Step Recovery is also the same no matter where one goes in the world. How can there be so much sameness in a world with so much differentness and diversity? I think this is one of the most powerful lessons to be learned from the culture of 12-Step recovery.

In 12-Step recovery, religion and spirituality are not necessarily one-and-the-same. Religion is seen as the practice of a set of beliefs about God and spirituality is simply a daily *personal relationship* with a Higher Power—God as *you* understand God. Prayer and meditation are the skills used to experience that daily personal relationship with one's Higher Power.

Remembering that each of us has our own "map of the world," which means there are over seven billion maps of spirituality out there, we can understand why we go out of our way to leave this a personal issue. The term "Higher Power" is meant to be a generic way of respecting individual preferences.

If you have any kind of faith or belief that there is a Higher Power looking out for all of us then ask yourself the following question: *"Would God want small children to believe that they are unlovable, unworthy of anything good in life?"* Would he want them to believe that they "can't do anything right" or that they "screw everything up?" Of course the answer to these questions would be no.

This is proof for the believer that the False Self we have come to know is a counterfeit because it is not what God created. The False Self is what life created, and it covered up most of what God created, submerging it deep beneath the surface of our awareness. God's creations have a purpose and a spirit. This is who we really are, our True Self, and it has been there since before our birth. We need to "recover" it.

I believe the True Self is who my Higher Power created and that this is where my spirit resides. I also believe this is why God feels especially far away to some. Our spirit is what connects with his Spirit. If we don't have access to our spirit, our True Self, we can feel cut-off from God. Our True Self is also where our purpose resides. In Rick Warren's book, *A Purpose Driven Life* (2002, 2007), the author points out that our purpose is not really our purpose at all … it is His purpose for us. We were created with a special set of talents and abilities in order to perform His purpose for us.

In the Bible, it says that *"He who overcomes himself is greater than he who overcomes a city."* Do you wonder which "self" we are to overcome? In another place, the Bible says, *"Blessed are those who mourn: for they shall be comforted."* Is *refusing to mourn* not what we do when we wear a mask, ignore our inner world, and pretend that everything is fine?

When God feels far away, could it be because our True Self, the part of us that connects with him, is buried so deep under the wounds of the False Self that we cannot feel His presence? If the answers to these questions are "yes," then turning our focus inward to surface and grieve our pain is the royal road to *true comfort and relief.* As we shall see in the next chapter, seeking comfort and relief in all the wrong places inevitably leads to more pain.

Even if you are agnostic, or atheist, for that matter, I think most can believe in the innocence of a child. We all come into this world innocent and pure. That innocent, pure True Self gets wounded and covered up by this world regardless of your religious or spiritual beliefs. For those of you who believe neither in God, nor in the inherent goodness of man, I may not have been able to provide sufficient proof of the True Self. If not, I challenge you to look within and see if it might be contempt and emotional wounds that are getting in your way. I believe in you and wish you all the wonderful things that life has to offer.

The next logical question is, *"How do we deal with this?"* Below is a description of what to look for when you …

... Discover your True Self!

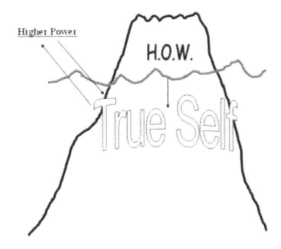

True Self / False Self

- Shares Authentic Self / Cover-Ups, Masks, Invented Self
- Loves Self & Others / False Self, Externally Focused
- Spontaneous, Energetic / Plans and Plods, Focused on Impression Management
- Expansive, Confident Contracting / "Shrinking," Fearful
- Giving, Communicating / Withholding, Non-Communicating
- Accepting of Self and Others / Envious, Critical, Idealizes,
- Accepts Mistakes as Learning / Perfectionistic
- Compassionate & Empathetic / Other-Oriented, Overly Conforming Or Good
- Boundaries & Self-Care / Self-Centered & All-About-Self
- Loves Unconditionally / Loves Conditionally

- Feels Feelings, Including Appropriate, / Denies or Hide Feelings,
- Including Spontaneous, Current Anger / Long-Held-Anger (Resentment)
- Open and Assertive / Aggressive, Passive, or Passive/Aggressive
- Intuitive, Rational, Logical / Magical thinking, Discounting, Illogical
- Loves to Play and Have Fun / Avoids Play, Fun or "Plays" addictively
- Healthy Vulnerability / Pretends Always to Be Strong or Perfect
- Powerful in the True Sense / Limited Power, a "Cover Up" for Protection
- Trusting / Distrusting or Naïve/Gullible
- Enjoys Being Nurtured / Avoids Being Nurtured
- Problem-Solves & Decides on Best Course of Action / Attacks, Retreats, or Surrenders
- Humble / Self-Deprecating or Self-
- Righteous
- Open to the Unconscious / Blocks Unconscious Material/feelings
- Remembers Our Oneness / Forgets Our Oneness; Feels too Separate
- Free to Grow / Gets stuck in repetitive cycles of Abandonment, Shame, and Contempt

3.1.1 Self-Preservation to Self-Actualization

Wouldn't it be great if we could go back and do our childhood over again knowing all we now know about childhood developmental dependency needs? And wouldn't it be great if we could heal our parents and teach them about this stuff, so they would create that safe container for us where we could concentrate on being happy, healthy kids instead of having to live in survival mode? Well, we may not have the magical powers to do that, but we do have some very powerful and amazing abilities to do something very much *like that*.

This section lays out a systematic approach for using a process called *Reparenting*. This approach teaches us a means of updating, re-educating, and re-imprinting the neural networks of survival and growth, with an emphasis on survival skills. The Reparenting process outlined here is used to focus on *precise locations* of survival-oriented networks to add new learning to those parts of self, thereby enhancing how they function.

Another goal is to soften the rigid boundaries between these fragmented parts of self by getting them to "communicate" with each other. We "think" and communicate with others using images, words, sounds, and gestures to express thoughts, ideas, beliefs and decisions. These are called cognitions. Neural networks in the mind-and-body communicate with each other using electrical and chemical (electro-chemical) forms of conveying data and information.

There is an amazing structure in the brain called the hypothalamus that, with help from other structures and systems such as the pituitary gland, converts *cognitive* information (thoughts, beliefs, etc.) into *bio-chemical* information (neurotransmitters, hormones, neuropeptides, etc.)–*this is how your psyche (mind) talks to your soma (body), and your body talks to your mind!*

This is also how some emotions can be destructive, either by creating a steady state of stress causing corrosive biochemical messengers like cortisol and adrenaline to flood the bloodstream or as they are converted into physical symptoms such as ulcers and migraines. An excellent technical book on this topic is *The Psychobiology of Mind-Body Healing*, by Ernest Rossi.

For now, just know that your "*psychology*" can communicate with your "*biology*" and that the body understands and responds to cognitions, especially metaphorical ones. We use this knowledge for good in devising therapies such as the Inner Child work and healing the Inner Family of Self.

To begin, let's look at some requirements, obstacles, and goals of *Inner Child Healing & Reparenting*:

3.1.2 Requirements of Adult/Child Recovery:

2. **Detachment/Dissociation** – The Adult ego state needs to be activated giving psychological distance in order to direct recovery for the Inner Children.

3. **Protection and Support** – The Inner Children must finally get their needs met by creating or activating a nurturing Inner Parent and Adult ego-state.

4. **Grieving** – The Inner Children need to be allowed to grieve their losses with support from the Inner Adult, Inner Parent and Higher Power.

3.1.3 Ways We Abandon our Inner Children:

1. **Avoiding Primary Feeling Words: Denying Feelings**
   - There are approximately seven primary feeling words: *angry/mad, sad, hurt, afraid/scared, lonely, shame/guilt, happy/glad.*

   - Most other feeling words are too ambiguous and adult-like for inner child work … they provide us with too much emotional and intellectual distance, something that impedes inner child healing.

2. **Hiding behind a Mask: Distracting from or Covering up Feelings**
   - The person often comes from the victim perspective and may even be crying, but the crying is usually learned behavior that has produced secondary gains in childhood; and may continue to produce such gains (i.e., attention, nurturing, and support).

- Expressing feelings from a persecutor or martyr perspective is quite different than expressing genuine anger or grief in relationship to the self. Roles such as these do not allow one to feel the authentic feelings that need to be expressed.

- *Hiding* so as to control and direct a conversation away from feelings.

- Constructing our lives in such a way as to never have a moment of down time. (External Focus to stay out of our feelings)

3. **Maintaining the Critical Inner Parent Voice:**
   - We learned to try to control our behavior and emotions using the same tools that were used by our parents–fear, guilt, and shame. Thus was born our critical parent voice that shames us and judges us, that beats us up and sabotages our ability to relax and enjoy life.

   - Personal empowerment involves making a decision to stop playing the victim, persecutor, and/or rescuer and a decision to learn how to live authentically in a recovery process.

4. **Allowing Abuse from Others**
   - We teach people how to treat us by setting or not setting healthy boundaries regarding what we will tolerate and then reinforcing those boundaries.

   - Creating healthy boundaries may be a skill we need to learn; a network we need to build because it either was not modeled well or not allowed at all in our families of origin.

- Children develop a neural network for accepting and living with abuse, sometimes to the extent that we will sabotage ourselves in adulthood when it looks like something good might be about to happen. (Self-Sabotage–positive intention is to avoid the pain of another disappointment by not allowing ourselves to hope again.)

3.1.4 Growth in Adult/Child Recovery:

1. We must recognize and quiet the Critical Inner Parent voice. We need to learn to notice the shaming, discounting, and disapproval patterns of our past and STOP hurtful criticism, replacing it with helpful respectful criticism when a critical thinking is required.

2. We must become our own Healthy Parent. We need to rescue, nurture and love our Inner Children—and STOP them from controlling our lives.

STOP them from driving the bus! Children are not supposed to drive; they are not supposed to be in control. When a child takes control, the Parent is supposed to step in and set limits.

Children are not supposed to be abused and abandoned. That's what caused our problems in the first place. Then we abandoned and abused our Inner Children by locking them in a deep, dark place within us and ignored them. When we get triggered, we let our Inner Children drive the bus–we let their wounds dictate our lives.

We must recognize and meet all the needs of our Inner Children by giving each of them the Time, Attention, Affection and Direction (Guidance and Discipline).

3.1.5 Goals of Adult/Child Work:

- This work is about becoming an integrated, whole, mature, adult person in action, in the way we live our lives and respond to life events and other people.

- The only way we can be whole is to own all parts of ourselves. By owning *all of the parts* we can then have choices about how we respond to life. By denying, hiding, disowning, and suppressing parts of ourselves we doom ourselves to *live life in reaction*.

- As long as we are reacting unconsciously out of a mass of unresolved abandonment, shame and contempt, it is nearly impossible to have any clarity about our inner life (i.e., Self-Awareness).

- It is vitally important to start separating out the different wounded parts of us, so that we can start healing the individual wounds/issues. That is the way we start to take power away from those wounds.

- When we have a strong emotional reaction to something or someone–when an emotional "button is pushed" and there is a lot of energy attached or a lot of intensity–It usually means there are unresolved emotional wounds from the past involved.

- It is one of the Inner Children that feels the panic or terror or rage or hopelessness or desperate loneliness, not the Adult.

- The more we can become aware of our "buttons," our emotional wounds, the more we can have some loving control over them instead of judging and shaming ourselves for our reactions.

- By searching out, getting acquainted with, owning the feelings of, and building a relationship with each of these "parts" or Inner Children, we can start being a loving parent to ourselves instead of an abusive one.

- We can set internal boundaries to:
  - **Protect** our Inner Children from the persecutor within/critical parent (be loving to ourselves);

○ **STOP** letting our childhood wounds control our life (we drive our own bus);

○ **Take responsibility** and own the truth of who we really are (*True Self*) so that we can open up to receive the love and joy we deserve.

3.2 Meet Your Inner Children

It has been said many times that one cannot have a good relationship with others, unless they first have a good relationship with themselves. And one cannot truly love another, unless they truly love themselves.

The following is a powerful method of sorting out and getting to know the inner family so that one can begin to develop more self-awareness, build rapport with their parts, and open the lines of communication between parts to initiate a healing process. All it requires is an active imagination, the ability to purposefully hallucinate without the use of drugs, and a desire to begin a new relationship with one's family of self.

You may want to look back and review Chapter 8 before beginning this exercise. A review of the Inner Child ego-states in that section will help with this part of setting up the Reparenting process. There is no right way to do this, I have never seen any two people do *Ego-State Projection* the same way—we all have unique maps of the world.

Exercise: Ego-State Projection – Get comfortable in a room with plenty of space, privacy, and at least six places to sit or stand. [Listen to the Ego-States Audio] OR…

- **Remind your Self** that there are five general ego-states within the Child ego-state:

○ Natural Child

o Little Professor
o Vulnerable/Needy Child
o Angry/Defiant Child
o Critical Parent (a child ego-state pretending to be a parent)

- **Now, imagine that you can ask** all five of these parts to come out and sit or stand anywhere they want in the room.

- **Ask yourself** who would be the first one to step out into the room? Use your intuition and just let it happen.

- **Notice everything you can** about the first part to come out into the room. Which one is it? Where is it sitting or standing? How is this part dressed? Notice the facial expression and body posture … what do those signs suggest about how this part feels? How do you feel in the presence of this part? Ask the part a question such as "How do you feel about being here right now?"

- **Do the same until you have all parts in the room.** Don't be surprised if a part is represented as a boy and another part as a girl. We all have a masculine side and a feminine side, plus there are gender-roles handed down by society that make certain behavior okay in a boy that's not ok in a girl and vice versa. Also don't be surprised if you get a sense that one or two parts are not willing to come forward. They may seem to be outside playing, or peeking in the doorway, or off riding a bike, or hiding somewhere.

- If you have difficulty getting one part to show up in the room it may be that you have disowned that part. Sometimes an Internalizer will "disown" or push out of awareness into the subconscious mind the Angry/Defiant Child. Externalizers have a tendency to disown their Vulnerable/Needy Child and so may have trouble visualizing that part of them. Just do the best you can to get as much participation as possible without forcing anything. In whatever way seems right for you.

- **Ask each part if it would like to pick a name** for itself; it may choose a nickname, a number, a feeling, anything it wants to be called. The important thing is to let the part pick the name.
- It may help to do this with a friend so they can guide you and you can focus on listening and observing with you intuition.

- **Finish up by drawing a picture of your Inner Children**. Sometimes it helps to draw two pictures; one when things are going well and one of when there are problems or stress.

Describe your Inner Family: Just document here what happened during your experience. There is no right way to do it–there is only what happens as you go through it. Get into as much detail as you can because there is nothing irrelevant about it. Where all the parts present? How did each of them feel about coming out into the room? How do they feel about each other? How do they feel about you? What does each of them want or need? (Don't be afraid to ask; they will answer questions through your intuition.)

_____

_____

_____

_____

_____

_____

_____

_____

_____

_____

_____

_____
_____
_____
_____
_____
_____
_____
_____
_____
_____
_____
_____
_____
_____

Once you have completed this _Ego-State projection exercise_ you have accomplished a very important step in sorting out and getting to know your "family of self" better. When these parts are in conflict with each other and all of them are inside your mind and body you have what is called _Simultaneous Incongruence_. Incongruence means "in conflict" or "out of synch" with each other. In other words, they are all running around inside making things hard to sort out, perhaps causing chaos and confusion.

When you project them out into the room, you have _Sequential Incongruence_. Some of them may still be in conflict with another part, and some may not know each other or even the Adult ego-state. However, now they are out in the room where you can work with them one at a time (sequentially), you can introduce them to each other (building cohesiveness and communication), you can ask them what they need or want (building rapport), and you can begin to get to know and take care of your parts (self-care).

3.2.1 Meet Your Ideal Parent/Adult Ego-State

In the above exercise, we have only met the Inner Children. All healthy inner families need a healthy, loving Parent ego-state and a well-adjusted Adult ego-state. For the purposes of healing it is wise to develop an imagined image of the *integrated, healed, healthy adult you* that you want to be in a few years. This *Ideal Self* acts as both healthy, loving parent *and* healthy well-adjusted Adult ego-states in concert with each other, integrated, but not completely fused into one ego-state.

It is important to remember the functions of these two ego-states as they are critical in the Reparenting process. **The Adult ego-state** may be thought of as the CEO of the self as it is responsible for executive functioning, which includes:

- Information gathering
- Computing (making sense out of the data gathered)
- Negotiation, mediation
- Strategic Planning
- Problem-Solving
- Decision-Making

The Parent ego state is the expert on how to parent, which includes two primary functions:

- Protection/Safety of children—Inner (self) and Outer (others)
- Nurturing the Inner family of self, Nurturing other loved ones.

The Child ego state, realm of the Inner Children, who are the experts for knowing:

- What I want.
- What I need.
- What I feel.

Being the CEO of the self, the Adult ego state is the part that "does business" with the outside world. In order to do that it must have open lines of communication with the other departments of self; i.e., the Parent and Child ego states. The Adult ego state must be able to remain objective, gather information from expert consultants (i.e., the Parent and Child ego states), interpret the data, compute by mixing the data together and visualizing the possible outcomes of certain decisions, anticipate and solve problems, then ultimately, make a decision. Once the decision is made it is also carried out from the Adult ego state in the ideal situation.

Exercise: Discover your Ideal Adult and Parent— [Listen to the Ideal Self Audio] OR Get comfortable again, go out into the future and imagine that you see yourself at somewhere between 18 and 24 months of recovery. This is the *Ideal You* ... the you that you want to be ... the you that doesn't get triggered nearly as much anymore ... the you that no longer "lives life in reaction" ... This is an image of your True Self emerging. When enough healing has occurred you will have clearly gotten in touch with this part of yourself.

Now imagine that this Ideal You steps into the room and chooses a location to sit or stand. Remind yourself that a healthy, loving Parent has the ability to nurture and protect the other ego-states, while the Adult ego-state provides all the executive functions such as those described above. This Ideal You can and does operate from either and/or both Parent and Adult ego-states as needed. This is the ego-state that will Reparent your inner children in the upcoming exercises while you (the current you) observes everything from *third position* as if a curious bystander. You become a witness to your own growth and healing process.

Sometimes the Ideal Self is a little hard to visualize at first. If this is the case you may want to borrow parts from your Higher Power, an admired adult in your past or current life, a mythical hero or TV adult/parent, or even the current adult you in a competent role at work or in some other activity you feel very good at. You can be as creative as you want in creating an Ideal You. You can even bring your Higher Power into the process when you need additional support; either by having Him there or just imagining what your Higher Power would say or do in the situation. And, last but not least, you can realize that the Ideal You is your *True Self*; the part that is connected to your Higher Power and as such, has knowledge of the truth to counter the false representations of the emotional wounds or *False Self*.

Describe your Ideal Adult and Parent Ego-states:

_____
_____
_____
_____
_____
_____
_____
_____
_____
_____

Exercise: Create Your Sanctuary [Listen to the Sanctuary Audio] OR…

A safe container is necessary for this work so, while you are at it, and since it money is no object, you might as well go all out and imagine the most awesome, incredible, magical place in the universe to be your sanctuary. Really spend some time on this and go all out. Perhaps you want to have a huge log home in the middle of a beautiful, flower-filled meadow, bordered by magnificent pine trees in the Rocky Mountains, or a beautiful home on your own private Fantasy Island with a white sandy beach and white-capped, deep blue ocean waves rolling in, or a penthouse suite on Park Avenue in New York City.

The only thing that matters is that this *Sanctuary* has everything all parts of your inner family could ever want and it's a safe place to work things out together. The inner children can have any favorite toys or pets from their past, they can have their own rooms with a magic door leading to any place they want to go every time they open it, like a favorite safe place or play place from the childhood. Let them help you create your sanctuary; and it can always be updated as needed. You can have a special huge bay window in the great-room that has any kind of view you want, such as a beautiful tropical waterfall one day, a lush green forest the next, and a view of a deep blue ocean the next day.

This room is the place you will meet with your inner family, spend time with and treat your inner children and build relationships between your different parts of self. This, in addition to all your other safety bubbles (meetings, sponsor, counselor, Higher Power, etc.) is where you will heal the abandonment, shame and contempt. Once it feels complete, let each of your Inner Children find their places in the Sanctuary. Let the Ideal Self explain to them that this is their new home and that the Ideal Self will stay with them and take care of them. The Sanctuary may be updated at any time, but as the Adult and Parent of the family, the Ideal Self makes the final decisions about that.

Describe your Sanctuary: Paint a "word picture" with as much sensory detail as you can. Better yet, get a sketch pad and draw a picture of it with vivid colors and details:

_____

_____

_____

_____

_____

_____

_____

_____

_____

_____

_____

_____

_____

_____

_____

_____

_____

3.3 Reparenting and Journaling

Why even spend time "digging up the past?" In reality, you don't have to dig up the past if you can relate to the issues outlined in this book. "The past" jumps up "out of nowhere" and slaps you in the face every time you "get triggered." These episodes cause child-created ego states to take over your life and "drive your bus" while you are trapped in the back seat holding on for dear life.

Whether it's the fight response (*Angry/Defiant Child*) or the flight response (*Vulnerable/Needy Child*) these parts of self end up hijacking your personality, causing wreckage in your life and havoc in your relationships. Reparenting is one of the most effective methods of healing these frozen feeling-states.

One of the most effective methods of Reparenting is a daily journal exercise. Writing tends to slow things down and help separate the parts of self enough to process triggering events and episodes as they occur. Most Inner Child and Adult/Child authors use a variation of journaling for this reason.

The following procedure is similar to and inspired by the procedure in Susan Anderson's book, *Journey from Abandonment to Healing*. Anderson's book focuses on healing through abandonment issues as they occur in the context of grieving the loss of love relationships. It is an excellent resource for those going through a break-up, divorce or other loss of love. As one might imagine, these situations are "trigger-rich" times in our lives and therefore, provide ample opportunities to do this healing work.

The purpose of daily journaling with the Inner Family-of-Self is twofold:

- **Self-Awareness:** To build relationships, rapport, and open lines of communication between the parts of self thereby softening the boundaries between them; this allows for integration (i.e., working in harmony).

- **Self-Care:** To provide care and "treatment" to the wounded parts of self as needed when they get triggered; this allows for healing and growth (i.e., integration).

Again, it has long been known that one cannot have healthy relationships with others until they first develop a healthy with themselves. A daily journal is not only an ideal way of accomplishing the two Reparenting objectives above, but it also provides one with an incredibly valuable resource–a record of the experience which can be used to identify patterns, triggers, what works, what doesn't work, and a visual history of progress.

3.3.1 A Basic Journaling Procedure

Set a time to journal every day even if it is only 15 minutes.

Make sure to keep your appointment with the Inner Family or you may increase the abandonment issues and fall out of rapport with one or more Inner Child.

Remember that the Inner Children are just like any other children; they need:

- Time
- Attention
- Affection
- Direction (Guidance & Discipline)

The Ideal Self is the part that leads the Reparenting process and provides all of the above needs.

The current you is present but only in *third position* (See page 196) unless the Ideal Parent or one of the children calls on the current you to participate.

Start by visualizing the room in the house where the meeting will usually occur and invite in the parts of self that want to participate. It may be that each Inner Child needs some one-on-one time with the Ideal Self and that may occur anywhere that Child wants in the sanctuary. Do not try to force any part to participate.

It is best that any dialog that takes place be written in the journal as it occurs. (See example below) Some people experience difficulty with this because of a past boundary violation where a parent or other person found and read their diary or other journal. It is not a hard and fast rule that things need to be written down, but it is helpful to have a record if possible.

In the early stages of journaling there is usually a "getting to know each other" period where the Ideal Self introduces him/herself, encourages the Inner children, one by one, to come in sit down, and let them know he/she wants to be there for them and take care of them now. Don't be surprised if one of more parts of self comes off as hostile. They may not trust you or your promise to "be there" for them. In that case maybe some apologies are in order and/or other amends needs to be made. (See example below)

In the next phases of the process the Ideal Self encourages the Inner Children to *talk about any triggers that occurred during the day*. There is usually more than one part involved in triggering events, encourage all involved to participate in the discussion, but with ground rules—only one talks at a time, no name-calling, shaming, etc. This is where healing opportunities present themselves and so, in this sense, triggering events are "good things" and are to be taken as a challenge rather than a disappointment. Below are the steps to take in helping the triggered part process the experience.

Get the triggered Child to *say everything he/she felt* during the episode.

If, as is usual, there is more than one *feeling,* process *those feelings one at a time*. It is tempting to jump in when the Child says "I felt hurt, sad, ignored, etc." and try to cheer them up...don't do that. Instead, encourage the Child to say everything he/she can about each feeling one at a time. This is about teaching emotional health which means to express the feelings completely to someone who cares enough to listen. Ask the following kinds of questions:

- *Tell me everything about the (hurt) ...*
- *I want to know everything about that feeling...*
- *What did you take that to mean? (elicit beliefs about the event)*
- *Now tell me about (the next feeling)*

Once the Child has said everything s/he can about each feeling now is the time to *tell the Child the TRUTH about him or herself* in that situation. The Ideal Self is the True Self and knows the Truth because it is the part that is connected to your Higher Power. The wounded Inner Children lived in the False Self and were exposed to Falsehoods…they need the truth from a caring Adult self they are learning to trust…you. Go through each feeling and tell the Child what it needs to know about the triggering event and/or other persons involved.

If no triggers occurred during the day, the Ideal Self gives time, attention, and affection and direction to build and strengthen relationships by asking each part how the day went and/or what each wants to do today. Perhaps the Children want to draw a picture of something they enjoyed doing in the sanctuary that day, or talk about something that happened in your outer world during the day that they liked or didn't like. Or maybe one or more parts wants to go on a fantasy outing with the Ideal Self like a horseback ride in the mountains, a hike in the woods, swimming at the beach, a ride in a hot-air balloon. Or maybe they all want to help plan your next vacation or weekend outing in the outer world—something they can enjoy along with you.

In the later stages of the process, the need to use the journal at all may naturally fall away because the whole process has become integrated as a subconscious program of internal communication. At this point self-awareness and inner processing has reached the advanced level where it is second nature. In this event, the fourth stage of learning, *unconscious competence*, has been accomplished. This in no way implies that one must give up the journal ... indeed, continue using it for the sake of having a record, or, if it remains valued by any part of you in other ways.

The ultimate goal of the Reparenting process is integration. In other words, to *thaw out the frozen feeling-states* helping them to grow into the present reality, to have access to the resourcefulness of the core self and to be able to fulfill their roles as part of the whole without the reactivity that resulted from the cycles of abandonment, shame, and contempt.

3.3.2 Example of a Journal Entry

The following example demonstrates how the dialog between your Ideal Self and Child ego states may look in your journal. Remember that when you begin this process, assuming you have never done this before, it is important to begin as if your family-of-self were meeting for the first time ... because they are.

And it may help to keep in mind that the wounded Child ego states may actually be like troubled foster kids who need lots of patience and guidance. They may even have a hostile tone at first.

Furthermore, all groups tend to "grope" around for a bit before they find the best procedure for them. Don't worry if things don't go well on the first attempt. If you get stuck re-read this chapter, discuss it with a recovery friend or sponsor, visit *the Forums* on my internet site (see footer below) and/or if you are in counseling ask your therapist for help.

Another very powerful way to get the conversation flowing is to write with your non-dominant hand when responding from one of the Children. Always use your dominant to write from the Idea Self perspective. The dominant hand is controlled by the dominant hemisphere of your brain (also identified as the location of executive functioning, i.e., thinking brain).

The non-dominant hemisphere is considered to be in control of emotional, intuitive, and instinctive functioning, i.e., the limbic brain. This would make the non-dominant side the home of the Inner Children and the dominant side the home of the Adult ego state. Some people are emotionally over-reactive because they tend to associate too easily, while others are emotionally numb because they dissociate too easily.

Use this technique to regulate feelings of safety, emotional intensity, and/or psychological distance. If it feels too intense back off and use your dominant hand all the way. If you get stuck try the technique. The following is an example of a first interaction:

Inner Child Journal Entry, Date: _____

True Self: "Hi everyone, thanks for coming today! My name is [Insert name of True Self] and I am from your future. I'd like to take care of you all so that we can be together and you won't have to feel bad or alone anymore."

Angry Child: "How do you know I feel bad? And what do you care anyway?!"

True Self: "I know I haven't been there for you [insert name of Angry Child] and I am sorry for that. I didn't really know what to do until now and I would really like another chance."

Angry Child: "Well, okay... I guess we can try."

True Self: "I wanted to ask you about something that happened today in that meeting at work. Do you remember the meeting?"

Angry Child: "Yes, that man Bill, was scaring [insert name of Vulnerable Child] when he got loud and bossy with you. I wanted you to tell him where to go!!"

True Self: "Oh...so you were protecting VC?"

Angry Child: "Yes, that's my job."

True Self: "AC do you mind if I talk to VC for a minute?"

Angry Child: "Okay."

True Self: "VC is AC right about you feeling scared today at the meeting?"

Vulnerable Child: "Yes."

Critical Parent: "This is so stupid! Just get over it and quit being a crybaby!!

True Self: "Okay [insert name of CP], I'm glad that you want to participate … I know you will be able to provide some very good input … Now, there are some ground rules I need to explain … To start with we don't interrupt each other and we don't call each other names here … okay?

Critical Parent: (grumbling under breath) "Okay!"

True Self: "VC tell me all about feeling scared at the meeting today."

Vulnerable Child: "It reminded me of those times when Dad would get mad and beat us." (starts to cry)

True Self: "Switches from Adult to Parent and is now holding VC in a rocking chair by the fireplace for a while as the other children watch ... then begins to explain, "Well, you need to know VC that I am here for all of you now and I am going to be handling things in the outer world from now on so you are not exposed to it. I want all of you to stay here in the Sanctuary where you are safe and let me handle things when they come up. Then we can talk about it later in the day when we meet like this … Okay? All the Children: "Okay."

3.3.3 Types of "Family Meetings"

The above example demonstrates a meeting of the Inner Family of Self on a *"triggering" day*, i.e., a day when emotional buttons get pushed to a degree that is out of proportion to the circumstances. There is an 80/20 rule spoken of in Inner Child work that says whenever one has an excessive emotional reaction, especially one that seems immature or out of proportion to the context after the fact, then 20% of that reaction is for the current context or situation, while the remaining 80% is from one of the Inner Children. A meeting as described above is ideal for those days when emotional reactivity has been present.

Not every day is a triggering day. In fact, there can be many days that are *"good days" or at least trigger-free*; especially the more one attends to their inner world of experience as with these daily meetings. On those days, it is just as important to have daily meetings. This is a time to spend time with the Inner Children and meet their needs for attention, affection, direction and fun. This is a *perfect way to build rapport and relationship within the family of self.*

For example, in the Sanctuary one may have a special door in the back of the house that opens out to any place in the world one would like to be. Perhaps when the meeting takes place, one or all Parts of Self wants to do something special or fun with you; you and your Parts could open the back door to a corral in a mountain meadow and go horseback riding, or open the door to an airport and go skydiving, or to a white sandy beach for a walk or parasailing adventure, or to anywhere your imagination can take you. At these times getting into a comfortable position, closing your eyes, and really getting into the imagery, sounds, fragrances, etc. will be useful. Mindfulness or other meditation skills may also come in handy for these times.

On some days there may be a lot of mixed feelings about a decision one must make. Ambivalence can become so strong that it paralyzes the person creating a feeling of being "stuck." At these times, a family meeting may start with an inventory of those mixed feelings, finding out which Part of Self is creating each feeling, having each Part explain their positive intention for creating the feeling, and then discuss as a group all their feelings and opinions about the decision. The Ideal Self gathers all the data, facilitates the discussion and mediates a group consensus by helping each Part to feel heard, understood, taken seriously and validated for having a positive intention. This must also include every attempt to meet the needs of all parts to the extent possible before making a decision.

Another type of meeting for the Family of Self is *the planning meeting. Perhaps a four-day weekend or annual vacation is coming up*. At such times, it is good to have a series of meetings to discuss who wants to do what and let all Parts in on the planning process. Many times this process leads to incredibly fun and relaxation vacation experiences whereas by ignoring the input of other Parts of self may lead to self-sabotage and bad vacation experiences.

The uses for these family meetings are only limited by the creativity and imagination of the family of self. Perhaps you don't have any idea what need to be the focus of the meeting so you have the Ideal Self ask *"What do we want or need to do today?"* Be sure to let all Parts give their input instead of taking the first suggestion that comes along.

3.3.4 Benefits of Daily Meetings

Going through the stages of learning something new is a bit cumbersome at first but daily practice of these techniques builds competence and results very quickly. What was once a jumbled mass of emotions or the chaotic "inner noise" some have referred to as *"the committee in my head"* that causes confusion, indecision, and feeling stuck soon becomes a coherent and productive inner dialog that happens quite naturally. This is called *"Self-Awareness"*—which is wonderfully liberating and productive.

Within a few weeks or months, you will no longer even need to wait to go home and journal (although it is highly recommended that you do continue for at least six months or longer, for the sake of a record if nothing else). You will eventually find yourself automatically having meetings in your mind with various Parts of Self, making decisions easily, clearing up hurt feelings, having productive self-talk, and generally being much more successful in the pursuit of happiness in all areas of your life.

3.3.5 Seven Step Feeling Process

When the Children can't wait for a meeting...

If, as a child, you were told you never did anything right, then as an adult you may react from the neural network of that child you were in the past. Likewise, if in your current relationship you find yourself haunted with the fear that your partner will leave you, you may be reacting to past experiences of abandonment from someone you love. These emotional and/or physical reactions are signals from your Inner Children. If you ignore the signals thinking you can deal with it later, but they intensify, it is usually because the feeling is being "turned up" by the Child—it can't wait until later because it has already been triggered.

Exercise: *Seven-Step Feeling Process for the Inner Child*
It is critical to learn to listen to these signals from your Inner Children. Most often the signals appear in the form of emotions, self-talk, intrusive images, or uncomfortable physical sensations. The self-talk and intrusive images have emotions attached in the form of physical sensations in the body. The following *Seven-Step Feeling Process* can be used to help you tune into these physical sensations and then learn to respond in a way that will soothe the inner Child and release the feelings.

1. **Notice the feeling or sensation.** You must first learn to notice the feeling, i.e., the uncomfortable physical sensation.

2. **Identify the location of the feeling or sensation**. Feelings usually reside in one of four major areas of the body; the jaw, neck and shoulders, chest, or stomach. Other parts of the body may also be involved but the center of it emanates from one of these major areas. Images and sounds may also accompany the signals.

3. **Breathe into that location** focusing all of your concentration on it and staying with that feeling or sensation. Experience it, allow it to exist, and ask it to communicate with you.

4. **Ask for and receive the message or positive intention** of the feeling or sensation. Remember that all parts of self and all feelings or sensations in our body have a positive intention for us. These signals or messages are meant to help us remain healthy and protect or preserve our body.

5. **Just relax, close your eyes, and ask** … *"Would the part of me responsible for this feeling in my stomach please tell me what is your message or positive intention for me."* Then, just wait for an intuitive reply to come to you. Ask more questions if you intuitively feel there is more to discover from this part of you.

6. **Express thanks and gratitude to the Child** for sending the communication.

7. **Now, make a 24-hour promise to that Child**. Tell the child that you intend to do something about this message within the next 24 hours. For instance, if the message received is that you're pushing yourself too hard, tell your child that you will take frequent breaks that day and spend time relaxing that evening by taking a bubble bath, watching a movie, or doing something fun.

Notice the feeling fade away. If your response to the child's message was adequate, the feeling will disappear. This is an indication that your response has been accepted and appreciated!

The Reparenting process outlined above is one that is specifically designed to fit with and address the issues outlined in this book. Explore the many books listed in Appendix A for more tools that will help in your unique journey of recovery. In fact, as mentioned earlier, one may not even want to begin with Reparenting at all. It may be more suitable for some to begin with a professional evaluation, engage in a therapeutic relationship, and deal with any "Tip-of-the-Iceberg" issues such as chronic addictions; first-things-first!

3.3.6 CBT Basics

Some people need to begin by bolstering their Adult ego-state so they can proceed with the Reparenting process. **Cognitive Behavioral Therapy** (CBT) is a great method for doing just that. CBT deals with limiting beliefs. If you read the previous chapter thoroughly, then you are now aware of the power of beliefs. Our example of the "Figure 8" below is a modification of a CBT tool applied to the Iceberg. Albert Ellis and Aaron Beck are widely known as the pioneers of CBT. They have their own variations in the theory and practice of CBT. Again, it is not our intent to go into the theory but simply to introduce you to the basics and provide some insight into how it may apply to changing our neural pathways. We will include a few more CBT interventions specific to addictions at the end of this chapter.

Basically, CBT presupposes that it's our *interpretation of events* ("B" in the *Figure 8*), rather than the events themselves ("A" in the *Figure 8*), that "trigger" the negative emotional and/or behavioral choices we make ("C" in the *Figure 8*) that we experience in a given situation. Here are the elements of subjective experience upon which CBT focuses:

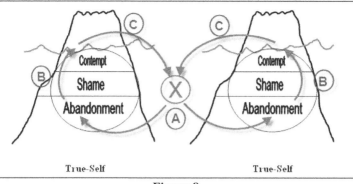

Figure 8

A = Activating event (Trigger)

B = Belief about the event (The mind-movie or meaning we make)

C1 = Emotional Consequence (Resulting emotional state of our movie)

C2 = Behavioral Consequence (Our actions or reactions to all of the above)

3.3.7 Automatic Negative Thoughts (ANTs)

As you can see above, our beliefs determines the movie or meaning we make of an incident which in turn determines our emotional state. Our resulting emotional state has an impact on the *actions* we choose or the *reactions* that seem to choose us. Our actions are *proactive choices* that we make about how to respond after first considering all the available options.

Our reactions are *reactive responses* that we act-out automatically when triggered. We often think of them as "buttons" to be pushed, as in, "So-and-so really pushes my buttons!" This reactivity is what keeps us stuck in cycles of destructive behavior because essentially we have "disowned" our choices in the matter.

Reactive responses are grounded in limiting or irrational beliefs, also known as cognitive distortions in CBT language. All the elements of these reactive buttons exist in our unconscious mind on well-established networks or programs that run automatically on cue; all the thoughts, beliefs, feelings, memories, self-talk, and even the physiology is part of the network.

Some limiting beliefs can be part of a system of beliefs, which are more difficult to change than a single limiting belief. CBT does not necessarily concern itself with why we have the beliefs or where they came from. Rather, it seeks to identify, dispute, and refute them, so they can be replaced with more accurate and rational beliefs. Once faulty beliefs are replaced the emotional state of the individual is more manageable and congruent with the situation in question.

In his book *Change Your Brain, Change Your Life,* Daniel Amen, MD, describes cognitive distortions as *Automatic Negative Thoughts*—"*ANTs*" for short. He paints a graphic picture when he suggests that we think of these automatic negative thoughts as little ants crawling around in our brain.

He takes the analogy further by reminding us what happens when we pick up an empty can or another container full of ants; they tend to crawl out of the container, onto our hands, up our arms, and as far as we will let them go. Usually we don't let them go very far before we begin brushing and flicking them off.

Dr. Amen suggests avoiding negative people because "their ANTs might mix with our ANTs and start mating and reproducing." The following is a list of common forms of cognitive distortions; i.e., mental and perceptual filters that result in limiting beliefs and skewed perceptions:

Automatic Negative Thoughts (ANTs)
- **Black-and-White Thinking** – Thinking in words like always, never, no one, everyone, every time, everything, etc.

- **Focusing on the Negative** – Filtering out the good, seeing only the bad in a situation, and magnifying it.

- **Fortune Telling** – Predicting the worst possible outcome to a situation. "Doing your pain in advance."

- **Mind Reading** – Believing that you know what others are thinking and feeling, even though they haven't told you.

- **Thinking With Your Feelings** – Believing negative feelings without ever questioning them … "I feel it, so it must be true." "If I *feel* stupid, I must *be* stupid."

- **Should/Must Thinking** – Thinking in words like should, must, ought, or have to … "Everyone should do things my way." "I ought to be able to control my feelings better." Don't "should" on yourself!

- **Self-Labeling** – Generalizing one or two qualities into a negative global judgment about you. You don't achieve your goal for two weeks in a row and say to yourself, "I'm a failure."

- **Personalizing** – Investing innocuous events with personal meaning. Thinking that things other people do or say is some kind of a reaction toward you.

- **Blaming** – Blaming someone else for your own pain/problems or go the other way and blame yourself for everyone else's problems.

- **Over-Generalizing** – Coming to a general conclusion based upon a single event or incident. Thinking that when one bad thing happens it is going to happen over and over again.

- **Catastrophizing** – Expecting disaster, going through the entire negative "what if's" in a situation.

- **Control Fallacies** – If you feel externally controlled, you see yourself as a helpless victim of fate. If you feel internally controlled, you see yourself as responsible for the pain and happiness of everyone around you.

- **Fallacy of Fairness** – You decide what is fair and feel resentful when other people don't agree with you.

- **Fallacy of Change** – You expect others to change to suit you if you could just pressure them enough. You need to change others because it seems that your hope for happiness depends entirely on them.

Adult-Oriented Cause-and-Effect Thinking

There are several methods of evaluating the quality of our beliefs to determine if they are useful to us. *Irrational beliefs* do not stand up to rational examination. Often, only a few questions will be enough to identify a limiting or irrational belief. Below are some questions from Neuro-Linguistic Programming and Rational Emotive Therapy that we can ask ourselves in order to strengthen the Adult ego-state and identify limiting beliefs that we may want to challenge or dispute:

NLP – The 4 Questions for Challenging Limiting Beliefs (Dilts)

1. How do you KNOW this belief is true?
2. What are the present and future positive benefits of holding this belief?

3. What are the present and future negative consequences of holding this belief?
4. What does this belief say about you? Others? The world?

RET – The 5 Rational Questions (Maultsby) (3 "no's" = *Irrational belief*)

1. Is my thinking here factual?
2. Will my think here best help me protect my life and health?
3. Will my thinking here best help me achieve my short-term and long-term goals?
4. Will my thinking here best help me avoid most undesirable conflicts with others?
5. Will my thinking here best help me feel the emotions I want to feel?

ANTs and the ABCs

If your beliefs do not stand up to the above tests, you can be sure they belong to a neural network that no longer serves you well. These old networks may have served a very important purpose at some other point in your life, but they need to be updated now. Once we identify the beliefs we want to change, we can begin to apply CBT and NLP techniques to make the desired change or, at a minimum, loosen their grip in preparation for change.

The examples below are some garden variety examples of change with CBT techniques for the sake of practice and acquiring skill. Changing strongly-held beliefs from the past will be a bit more of a challenge. It is always best to start with garden variety examples when learning something new; first develop the skill and then move on to more advanced challenges.

Example #1

A = Activating Event: Hear a loud noise while sleeping

B = Belief about the Event: Movie of someone breaking in (Catastrophizing)

C1 = Emotional Consequence: Panic and Fear

C2 = Behavioral Consequence: Call the police who come out and find a cat knocked something over on the back porch

CHANGE OF BELIEF changes everything but the activating event…

A = Activating Event: Hear a loud noise while sleeping

B = Belief about the Event: Change Channels: Movie of "don't do your pain in advance... It could be anything"

C1 = Emotional Consequence: Normal anxiety, no panic

C2 = Behavioral Consequence: Carry a big stick and go check it out... find a cat knocked something over on the back porch

Example #2

A = Activating Event: someone giggles while you are sharing your thoughts at a meeting

B = Belief about the Event: Movie soundtrack of "they are laughing at me" (Personalizing)

C1 = Emotional Consequence: Anxiety and humiliation

C2 = Behavioral Consequence: abruptly stop talking and shut down without finishing your thoughts, everyone wonders what's wrong

CHANGE OF BELIEF Changes everything but the activating event…

A = Activating Event: someone giggles while you are sharing your thoughts at a meeting

B = Belief about the Event: Change channels to Movie of "I wonder what they are thinking about … That's pretty rude …"

C1 = Emotional Consequence: Curiosity and normal annoyance

C2 = Behavioral Consequence: Go on talking and finishing your thoughts, not an issue

Appendix A
Therapy Handouts

Appendix B
Feelings

Appendix C
Signs & Symptoms of Codependency

Appendix D
Other Books, Programs, & Services by Don

A Hero's Journey

In 1968 Joseph Campbell wanted to know what it took to be a "hero" so he studied all the stories he could find about real-life and mythical heroes. He found that there was indeed a theme, so he wrote an essay about it. He named it *A Hero's Journey*.

I like this model as a way to describe the journey of recovery; whether it's recovery from addiction, codependency, Adult/Child Syndrome, or any other chronic condition. Especially in the early stages recovery is truly a heroic journey! Below is my take on *A Hero's Journey* as it relates to 12-Step recovery:

1. Hear a Calling—Through an event referred to as the "wake-up call" or "hitting bottom" our hero first "hears their calling" to change.

2. Accept the Call—Ignoring the calling causes the symptoms or problem to intensify ... until acceptance of the calling is the only option left.

3. Crossing the Threshold—Deciding to step out of one's "comfort zone" (familiar old life) and into "recovery" (awkward new life) with the help of mentors and other supports. A good analogy for what this is like is to imagine finding yourself in a foreign land where you know nothing about the language, social norms, or culture—you would need a guide, mentors, or teachers to teach you the language and show you the way.

4. Facing Your "Demons"—With the help of your new mentors and friends who have been-there-and-done-that ... facing your fears, cycles of abandonment, shame or contempt, and other unhealthy behavioral and emotional patterns that keep you stuck in the problem.

5. Transform Your "Demons"—The spiritual development in recovery leads to powerful new coping skills, self-awareness, and principles for living that help you overcome what seemed impossible to overcome before. The new recovery skills replace the old survival skills that are no longer helpful or necessary.

6. Fulfill the Calling—As a result of this journey, a fulfilling, successful way of life that fulfills the calling replaces the old painful way of life—A new "comfort zone" is achieved.

7. Homecoming—Carrying the message of hope back home and pass on what you have learned to others that are stuck in a similar way. You must give it away in order to keep it.

ABCs and the Figure 8

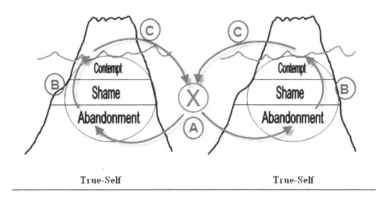

A = Activating Event: (Sensory Facts) *"What happened?"* (X)

Foreground: Describe the event in sensory terms: what did you SEE and what did you HEAR in *your outer world?*

Background: In *your inner world,* what memories, images, sounds, and physical sensations did this event remind you of – if any? In what context did X occur; *what mood were you in at the time, what things were going on during the past few hours or days prior to this event, were you under stress, etc.?*

B = Beliefs about Event: *"What did you take it to mean?"* What *Automatic Negative Thoughts* (See ANT's Handout), *limiting beliefs*, and *negative self-talk* about the Activating Event (X) did you experience? What Part "was driving the bus": Was it the Angry/Defiant Part, Vulnerable/Needy Part, Critical Parent, Little Professor, or another part that made the meaning? Was more than one part involved?

C1 = Emotional Consequences of Beliefs: *How did you react* emotionally *when you had these thoughts?*

- What emotions did you experience when you thought these things? (Angry, Sad, Scared, Guilty, Ashamed, Glad?)
- How did you feel about having these feelings at the time?

C2 = Behavioral Consequences of Beliefs: *How did you react* behaviorally *when you had these thoughts and feelings?*

- What actions did you take as a result of these beliefs?
- How did you treat yourself and/or others in reaction to these beliefs?
- What addictions/obsessions did you experience in reaction to these beliefs?
- How did you feel about these actions and reactions after it was all over?

The Figure 8 Journaling Format

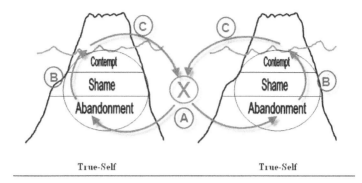

A = Activating Event: (Sensory Facts) *"What happened?"*
(X)

Foreground:

Background:

B = Beliefs about Event: *"What did you take it to mean?"*

Parts Involved:

C1 = Emotional Consequences of Beliefs: *"What did you feel in response to these thoughts?"* (Angry, Sad, Scared, Guilty, Ashamed, Glad)

C2 = Behavioral Consequences of Beliefs: *"What did you do in response to these thoughts and feelings?"*

Results: *How did the other person respond to what you did (your C2)?*

D = Disputation: *Who or what would you be without these thoughts and ideas?*

Identify any ANTs (pp. 212-214) above and use you Adult ego-state to develop an accurate, objective, cause-and-effect disputation of the distorted thinking:

What new self-talk, thoughts, and beliefs do you now choose to attribute to these types of events based upon the above results:

E = Effect of the Disputation: Now take a moment to close your eyes and observe the ideal "you" responding in these new ways:

What emotions can you now experience with these new thoughts/beliefs?

How do you treat yourself and/or others with these new thoughts/beliefs?

Do you like who you are with these new thoughts/beliefs? Is this "you"?

Compound Script Decisions:

1. Identify a Script Message (Injunction)

_____

(Don't…)

2. Determine the Script Decision

_____

(I mustn't…)

3. Identify observations that the Little Professor may have used back then to override the Script Decision.

"Dad/Mom/Others seem to highly value or want me to

_____ _"_

(Observation)

_"Therefore, I or it (prohibited behavior) may be acceptable so long as _____ "_

(Counter Injunction)

4. Identify the Compound Decision by combining the Injunction with the Counter Injunction:

_"I can _____ so long as I_

(Response to Item #1)

_____ "_

(Counter Injunction—above)

5. Identify the feelings & sensations you experience when you don't perform the counter-Injunction:

_"When/if I don't _____ I_

(Counter Injunction)

_feel _____ "_   (Scripty Feelings)

Grief Work and Adult/Child Recovery

Grief work and Adult/Child recovery often go hand-in-hand because growing up in a less-than-nurturing family system means multiple losses—loss of relationships, loss of love, and loss of identity—in general, loss of "the way things were supposed to be." In order to look at the relationship between grief and Adult Child Syndrome it would be best to first look at the most well-known and widely accepted model of the grief process—that being the model outlined by Dr. Elizabeth Kubler-Ross in her landmark book *On Death and Dying.* Dr. Kubler-Ross wrote this book as a study of how people handle death and dying. It was later found that the stages she outlined are typically seen in any loss-related experience. Abandonment issues and unmet dependency needs in childhood are serious loss-related issues.

Children in dysfunctional families not only suffer many losses—they also have no real emotional support in order to teach them how to grieve those losses. In fact, the teaching they do get is usually the opposite of what they need, i.e., "don't talk and don't feel" family rules, either spoken or unspoken.

This teaches them to thwart the grief process by stuffing the emotions. As the losses begin to pile up it becomes like a log jam in a stream or river ... they just keep piling up causing the emotional stream to stay constantly at flood stage. In other words, every time there is another loss, the person with complicated and unresolved grief is put in touch with all those unfinished grief episodes causing an extra strong reaction to the current loss.

Here are the five stages of grief as outlined by Kubler-Ross:

1. **Denial**—A "shock absorber for the soul"
2. **Anger/Guilt**—Anger if turned outward, and guilt if turned inward.
3. **Bargaining**—usually in the form of *"if...then"* statements
4. **Mourning**—Grief related depression
5. **Acceptance**—a return to somewhere near the pre-loss level of functioning.

- **Stage One, Denial**, is normal and necessary as it allows the reality of the loss to "sink in" at a suitable pace for grief work—unless one gets stuck in denial as with addictions.

- **Stage two, Anger/Guilt,** is a signal that the person is allowing the loss to sink in and progressing toward acceptance of the loss—and they don't like it! So they get angry at whoever is available. When Adult-Child Syndrome is present this is where the *Angry/Defiant Child* ego-state can jump up and "drive the bus" for a while. Some people need a shoulder to cry on, but the *Angry/Defiant Child* needs an arm to punch.

- **Stage Three, Bargaining,** is usually in the form of an "if, then" statement: "If we go to counseling then maybe we can save this marriage," or, "If I go into treatment then maybe they'll teach me to drink responsibly." As we can see with these examples, sometimes bargaining is helpful, sometimes hurtful—but it is always creative because this is the work of the Little Professor ego-state when Adult/Child issues are at play.

The Little Professor is the part of the Child ego-state that has always been in charge of figuring out how to minimize the pain of not getting needs met. This creativity can be a person's best asset or worst liability—depending on how it is used.

- **Stage Four, Mourning,** is the stage that is closest to acceptance of the realities associated with the loss. Human beings have a need to give testimony to the importance of a relationship though outward expression and demonstration of pain when that relationship is lost. Stage Four is the territory of the *Vulnerable/Needy Child* ego-state. In a dysfunctional family the first seven years of life are when the child is the most vulnerable and needy. It is also when they accumulate and carry most of the original pain of abandonment. It is the part of self that comes to the surface—bringing with it all the unfinished losses of the past—anytime a loss or even a threat of impending loss is present.

- **Stage Five, Acceptance.** This is the end-stage of grief work. If you imagine there is an attachment—like a rope or a cable—between the love object and the person then you will have an idea of the purpose of grief. Grief helps one break the bond, say good-bye, and let go—keeping the good memories and moving on with life.

If you have ever seen a rope or a cable break then you know it doesn't break all at once—in a painful process it slowly unravels until the core strands are present (Stage Four) and then it breaks leading to stage five: Acceptance of the loss.

Complicated or Unfinished Grief

Adult/Children rarely allow the grief process to get that to the Acceptance Stage. That's why they have a "log-jam" of grief issues waiting to be dealt with early in the recovery process. The *Angry Child* frequently comes out first mad at the world, mad at the object of the loss, or turning the anger inward—mad at self (guilt). The *Little Professor* gets busy trying to find a way to hold on and not have to go through the process. When triggered, or allowed to surface, the *Vulnerable Child* brings all the original pain and fear into awareness— perhaps even a sense of panic. A person may bounce around from one stage to another in a chaotic fashion until they find a way to stuff the current loss in on top of the other losses—or release it in recovery.

A *"safe container"* is required for Adult/Child Recovery to proceed. This safe container is created through building the internal and external supports necessary to provide an adequate structure. *External supports* include sponsors, counselors, 12-Step groups, church groups, etc. *Internal supports* include self-awareness, an internal *"loving Parent,"* a *Higher Power*, an inner sanctuary or safe place, and new coping skills to use in place of old survival skills.

Cop-Out Language Patterns

"Try" – Children learn to say "try" in order to get their parents off their backs. (passive defiance). In this case, the thing never gets done because the person was "unable" to do it (see "Can't"). A more appropriate use of the word is to "attempt/experiment to see if I like it."

"Can't" – This is a substitute for the word "won't" which is the most appropriate word in over 90% of the cases when someone says "I can't." To say I can't do something usually discounts our adult resources and free will. The appropriate use of the word "can't" is when we are not trained or do not otherwise possess the necessary skills or abilities to do the thing in question. When we have the abilities then not doing the thing is now a choice we make—therefore, "I won't" do it.

"Make Feel Myth" –It is in the magical thinking of childhood that we learn to say someone "made me feel" a certain way. In fact, we are trained to think that way— *"Now when we get there be sure to eat all of Grandma's dumplings so you don't make her feel bad,"* or *"I never would have hit you if you didn't make me so mad today!"*

A good example is when someone has a flying phobia and says "Planes scare me!" –Planes don't scare people, and flying doesn't scare people. They scare themselves with the disaster movies they are playing in their own mind. A child can be made to feel because they don't have the abstract thinking abilities, strength to protect themselves, and other resources of an adult. A six year old is not able to say to themselves– *"Wow, Dad's drinking problem is really getting out of hand. If I don't do something this may start to affect my self esteem. I think I'll just move in with the Jones' down the street for a while."*

When we get triggered into our child-created ego-states we can lose touch with our adult resources and *feel* as helpless as that younger version of ourselves. But the truth is that when we learn grounding and centering skills, we can maintain our adult freedoms and abilities.

Substituting "It" for "I" –Putting "it" in place of "I" is a way of disowning or discounting responsibility for our decisions, choices, and feelings. Some people refuse to accept credit by saying something like, *"It* was fine until *I* forgot what to say and messed the speech up."* Other people refuse to accept accountability by saying something like *"I* was giving a great presentation until *it* got all messed up."* Some people tend to depress themselves by using "I" for self-persecution and "it" to disown self-praise. Next time you hear yourself say something like *"If I don't work hard, 'it' doesn't count,"* replace the "it" with "I" and see if that feels true. If it does, you may have discovered the roots of your work-a-holism.

Nurturing Parent Exercise

1. Make a list of 10 adjectives that describe what you think is an ideal Nurturing Parent. *(e.g: warm, soft, loving, caring, protective, accepting, etc.)*

     1.

     2.

     3.

     4.

     5.

     6.

     7.

     8.

     9.

     10.

2. Write up to ten things you would like to hear from your ideal Nurturing Parent. Perhaps things you longed to hear from your own parents. (*e.g., "I love you," "Enjoy yourself," "don't worry, I am here for you," "I will protect you," I'm glad you're my son/daughter," etc.*)

1.

2.

3.

4.

5.

6.

7.

8.

9.

10.

3. Record these new "Permissions" and Affirmation onto a CD, blend with meditation or other relaxation music and listen each day. Or have someone create an affirmation CD for you!

Appendix B
List of Feelings

Abandoned	Disappointed	Insulted	Reassured
Affectionate	Disgusted	Intimidated	Refreshed
Afraid	Distracted	Irritated	Rejected
Alone	Distressed	Isolated	Relaxed
Ambivalent	Disturbed	Jealous	Relieved
Angry	Dominated	Jilted	Reluctant
Annoyed	Divided	Joyous	Remorse
Anxious	Doubtful	Jumpy	Resigned
Apathetic	Eager	Kind	Resistant
Appalled	Ecstatic	Lazy	Responsive
Ashamed	Embarrassed	Left Out	Restless
Assertive	Empathetic	Lonely	Ridiculous
Astounded	Empty	Longing	
	Enraged	Lost	Sad
Bad	Envious	Love	Satisfied
Betrayed	Excited	Loving	Scared
Bitter	Exhausted	Lovable	Serious
Bold	Exploited	Low	Shocked
Bored	Fascinated		Shame
Brave	Fear	Mad	Shy
Burdened	Flustered	Mean	Silly
	Foolish	Melancholy	Skeptical
Calm	Fortunate	Miserable	Sneaky
Challenged	Frantic	Nervous	Solemn
Cheated	Frustrated	Nice	Sorrowful
Cheerful	Frightened	Numb	Spiteful
Clever	Furious	Obnoxious	Stingy
Competitive	Glad	Obsessed	Strange
Concerned	Good	Odd	Stunned
Condemned	Gratitude	Open	Surprised
Confident	Grief	Outraged	Sympathetic
Confused	Guilty	Overjoyed	Tempted
Conspicuous	Happy		Tense
Contempt	Harassed	Pain	Terrible
Contented	Hate	Panic	Terrified
Cruel	Hatred	Passive	Threatened
Crushed	Helpful	Peaceful	Trapped
Curious	Helpless	Persecuted	Troubled
Defeated	Homesick	Petrified	Uneasy
Defensive	Hopeful	Pity	Unfortunate
Delighted	Horrible	Pleasant	Unwilling
Depressed	Hurt	Pleased	Vulnerable
Deserted	Hysterical	Powerful	
Desolate	Ignored	Powerless	Weak
Despair	Impressed	Pressured	Willing
Detest	Indignant	Proud	Willful
Devastated	Infatuated	Puzzled	Wonder
Different	Inspired		Worry

Appendix C
Codependent Traits & Patterns

These patterns and characteristics are offered as a tool to aid in self-evaluation. They may be particularly helpful to newcomers. Circle the question number for each "yes" answer.

Denial Patterns:

1. I have difficulty identifying what I am feeling.
2. I minimize, alter or deny how I truly feel.
3. I perceive myself as unselfish and dedicated to the well-being of others.

Low Self Esteem Patterns:

1. I have difficulty making decisions.
2. I judge everything I think, say or do harshly, as never "good enough."
3. I am embarrassed to receive recognition and praise or gifts.
4. I do not ask others to meet my needs or desires.
5. I value others' approval of my thinking, feelings and behavior over my own.
6. I do not perceive myself as a lovable or worthwhile person.

Compliance Patterns:

1. I compromise my own values and integrity to avoid rejection or others' anger.
2. I am very sensitive to how others are feeling and feel the same.
3. I am extremely loyal, remaining in harmful situations too long.

4. I value others' opinions and feelings more than my own and am afraid to express differing opinions and feelings of my own.
5. I put aside my own interests and hobbies in order to do what others want.
6. I accept sex when I want love.

Control Patterns:

1. I believe most other people are incapable of taking care of themselves.
2. I attempt to convince others of what they "should" think and how they "truly" feel.
3. I become resentful when others will not let me help them.
4. I freely offer others advice and directions without being asked.
5. I lavish gifts and favors on those I care about.
6. I use sex to gain approval and acceptance.
7. I have to be "needed" in order to have a relationship with others.

These Patterns and Characteristics of Codependence are reprinted from the website www.CoDA.org with permission of Co-Dependents Anonymous, Inc. (CoDA, Inc). Permission to reprint this material does not mean that CoDA, Inc. has reviewed or approved the contents of this publication, or that CoDA, Inc. agrees with the views expressed herein. Co-Dependents Anonymous is a fellowship of men and women whose common purpose is to develop healthy relationships and is not affiliated with any other 12-Step program.

Appendix D
Other Books, Programs, and Services by Don Carter

Books:
Thaw – Freedom from Frozen Feelings
Thawing Childhood Abandonment Issues
Thawing Your Relationships

Websites:
Internet-of-the-Mind.com
Hundreds of pages of information about therapy

Oasis-Connections.com
Don's membership web site loaded with resources,
downloads, coaching services, social network, chat rooms,
and online versions of the *Thawing the Iceberg Series*

Don-Carter.com
Carter Counseling & Coaching Services web site
Request an appointment and information about services

Online Coaching Services:
Contact Don through one of his web sites or
By calling (573) 634-2254 to discuss the coaching process
and see if it may fit for you

Counseling Services:
Contact Don through one of his web sites or
by calling (573) 634-2254 to discuss the counseling process
or to arrange an appointment

Made in the
USA
Middletown, DE